The Student Practitioner in Early Childhood Studies

The Stud   *working*
with chil   l Studies
students   ating to
young ch

With us   ers track
their acac   e degree
programn

- prepa
- provi
- devel   lational
  pedag
- provi   wledge,
  skills,   ren and
  adults

Fully supp   l think-
ing, this he   manner.
The autho   dagogy,
confidence   opment
and emplc   book is
essential re

Ruby Oate   s, Early
Childhood

Christine H   ramme
at the University of Derby, UK, and an early years' teacher.

The Student Practitioner in Early Childhood Studies

An essential guide to working with children

Edited by Ruby Oates
and Christine Hey

Routledge
Taylor & Francis Group

LONDON AND NEW YORK

First published 2014
by Routledge
2 Park Square, Milton Park, Abingdon, Oxon OX14 4RN

and by Routledge
711 Third Avenue, New York, NY 10017

Routledge is an imprint of the Taylor & Francis Group, an informa business

British Library Cataloguing in Publication Data
A catalogue record for this book is available from the British Library

Library of Congress Cataloging-in-Publication Data
The student-practitioner in early childhood studies : an essential guide
   to working with children / edited by Ruby Oates, Christine Hey.
      pages cm
   Includes bibliographical references.
   1. Early childhood teachers—Training of.   I. Oates, Ruby.   II. Hey,
Christine.
   LB1732.3.S78 2014
   372.21—dc23
   2013040176

ISBN: 978-0-415-71925-4 (hbk)
ISBN: 978-0-415-71924-7 (pbk)
ISBN: 978-1-315-78117-4 (ebk)

Typeset in Sabon
by Apex CoVantage, LLC

Printed and bound in Great Britain by
TJ International Ltd, Padstow, Cornwall

Contents

Contributors

Michelle Appleby is a former primary school teacher in the United States specialising in science and creative arts. She is currently a senior lecturer on the BA (Hons) Education Studies degree as well as one of the senior academic counsellors for the Joint Honours Scheme at the University of Derby. Michelle teaches a module critiquing the use of psychometric and standardised testing in the field of education. She is currently undertaking doctoral-level research investigating the motivating factors of students engaging in a joint honours degree and the achievement levels of these students. Her other research interests include literacy development, international and comparative education, alternative forms of education, the psychology of learning and social development throughout life and understanding and managing behaviour in a learning environment.

Christine Hey is an early years' teacher and lecturer. She is particularly interested in the opportunities that settings provide for early language acquisition and development, with an emphasis on real experiences and the vocabulary that these offer. In a varied career as nursery teacher, infant teacher, peripatetic special needs teacher and SENCO, Christine retains an interest in inclusive policies and practice and the importance of understanding legislation to inform respectful inclusive practice. A fellow of the Higher Education Academy, she currently lectures on the BA (Hons) Early Childhood Studies at the University of Derby, UK, and teaches in the Foundation Stage.

Ruby Oates is an assistant subject head in the School of Education & Social Science at the University of Derby, with particular responsibility for the BA (Hons) Early Childhood Studies and BA (Hons) Education Studies degree programmes. Ruby qualified as a teacher in 1983, specialising in the social sciences. She was head of Early Years at a North Nottinghamshire college of further education for ten years and played a key role in the development and growth of early childhood education and care qualifications. Ruby's doctoral thesis captured the voices of early years' practitioners in the workplace during a period of professionalization. Her interests include women's position in the workplace and the sociology of childhood.

Andrew Sanders is a former practitioner and manager of early years' settings. With a particular interest in new perspectives and approaches to learning, teaching and assessment, among other arenas, Andrew is involved in virtual communications, innovative vehicles for student involvement, 'accessible writing' and studies of the notion of childhood over time, place and culture. He is also involved in collaborative ventures and working in learning partnerships with other higher education establishments. A fellow of the Higher Education Academy, he currently lectures in a range of disciplines on the BA (Hons) Early Childhood Studies at the University of Derby, UK.

Robin Sedgwick has been teaching for over forty years in a variety of settings, including a grammar school, an inner-city comprehensive and two further education colleges. He currently teaches on the BA (Hons) Early Childhood Studies degree at the University of Derby, where he has developed and delivered the Self-Management and Study Skills module taken by all new entrants to the programme.

Helen Simmons is a childhood studies graduate with a master's degree in education studies; she has significant experience in working in nurseries and as a private nanny. Before joining the BA (Hons) Early Childhood Studies team at Derby, Helen taught vocational early years courses in a further education college in Coventry. Helen has undertaken recent research into leadership in the early years, and as a doctorate student she has a particular interest in the social and cultural pressures new parents face. Helen lectures across all levels of the degree, with specialisms including the development of children aged 0–3 years, well-being from birth and leadership in the early years.

Jon White qualified as a teacher in 1978 and first taught in a boys' secondary modern social priority school. Following six years with the Department of Defence, he took up a position as head of biology in a large inner-city comprehensive school. Combining this post with working with children and adults in a range of environments, he undertook a master's degree, with a focus on the management of change in children's lives. As a senior lecturer at the University of Derby, he teaches on a variety of modules on the BA (Hons) Early Childhood Studies programme and leads the MA (Ed) Early Years pathway. He is involved with a variety of research projects, both in the university and across Europe.

Ellen Yates is a former primary teacher with experience in working with children across the 3–11 age range in a number of school settings in central London and Derby City. Ellen also has international experience and spent five years in Malaysia establishing the early years' departments in two large international schools. Her current interests include creativity, play and children's literature and the role of leadership in effective practice. In her spare time Ellen works with ceramics and has a studio in Derby city. Ellen is a fellow of the Higher Education Academy and lectures on the BA (Hons) Early Childhood Studies Degree at the University of Derby, UK.

Introduction

Ruby Oates and Christine Hey

Welcome to *The Student Practitioner in Early Childhood Studies: An essential guide to working with children.*

This textbook is both an offering and a response; as the former, it seeks to offer an alternative view of early childhood studies by approaching the discipline from the perspective of a student practitioner, and as the latter aim, this text arises from and is informed by many encounters between students, tutors and placement supervisors. To this end, the editors wanted to provide a textbook that answered many of the questions which students have and which also responds to a diverse range of knowledge and experience; from students who arrive with GCSE 'A' levels but no knowledge of children and settings, to students with a wealth of practice experience who are seeking a firmer grounding in theory and current research.

Our conversations have highlighted how confusing the early years' sector can be to learners as they try to navigate a world of relationships, social interactions, policies, processes and procedures.

The eight chapters, therefore, support you, as an early childhood studies student, through your studies, building on your emerging knowledge and confidence, offering guidance to secure reflective practice while also asking you to acknowledge and reflect upon your academic studies alongside your development as a practitioner.

The editors acknowledge the critical role politics and policy play in early childhood and its provision and also recognise the transient nature of much policy and how it can be challenging in practice. Therefore, this text is focused on your role as a student practitioner who is a thinker and a reflective enabler; responsive, articulate, knowledgeable, ethical and confident of your advocacy of children's needs and rights. This flexibility allows you to respond appropriately and questioningly to the shifting world of early childhood policy and practice, rather than being overwhelmed by it.

Central to this textbook is the notion, discussed in Oates *et al.* (in Papatheodorou and Moyles [2009]) of the small spaces, those critical moments and interactions that underpin a young child's experiences in the early years' setting. You, the student practitioner, are reminded throughout this textbook of the vulnerability and value of relationships, the importance of communication, respect, ethical values and an ethos that places the child in the centre of your practice.

From the moment of arriving at the beginning of your learning journey, through your emerging and developing practice to becoming a professional, researcher and potential future leader, you are encouraged to recognise that central to this journey is communication and the relationships that are forged between practitioners and children. It is our belief that the quality of these relationships and social interactions underpin an enabling environment in which young children may thrive.

In each chapter, you are provided with activities and opportunities to reflect upon your own practice and studies. A flag indicates where you may link the activity to your academic studies; this supports the notion of theory and practice working together.

Each chapter provides a range of suggestions for further reading to extend your understanding and knowledge, recognising that the discipline of early childhood studies is wide and ever increasing.

Chapter One will introduce you to teaching and learning in university and supports you in getting the most from university by utilising support systems, personal and academic tutors, subject library support, student support services, peer mentoring, learning support and career development. It supports your information-finding skills and introduces you to sourcing academic and non-academic resources, including library collections, journals, web-based sources, and the university networked system and virtual learning environment. You will learn what constitutes a reliable source and how to select these. It provides guidance on key issues of academic presentation, plagiarism, citations and referencing, as well as introducing a variety of information styles such as reports, essays and presentations.

Chapter Two introduces you to a range of research methodologies, an understanding of the ethical issues related to research and an introduction to different research paradigms and how these influence methodological choices. It starts from the basis that all early childhood studies students are researchers from the moment they undertake their practice experience – for example, in the first year when undertaking child observations. It introduces the student to a range of qualitative and quantitative methods and strategies for carrying out research and provides you with skills to undertake a literature review.

Chapter Three explores the notion of an emerging practitioner, highlighting the importance of preparation, participation and observations in practice. Further supporting the student practitioner in what may be your first early years' placement, it also offers strategies for successful observations and an exploration of appropriate, professional conduct and presentation. As noted in the introduction, this chapter recognises the diverse experiences of students entering higher education.

Chapter Four builds on the previous chapter, reprising some key elements of preparation and professionalism. It provides support and guidance for managing placement issues and also how to successfully manage academic studies in placement. It recognises the debt that students owe to placements in supporting their studies but also acknowledges that not all placement experiences are successful, and offers tips to support students in a range of circumstances. It introduces the notion of reflective practice, exploring strategies and reasons for reflection, building upon your increased ability to observe and make sense of what you experience in placement.

Chapter Five explores how students can become enabling practitioners. It suggests different ways of seeing enabling environments and what these may look like. The chapter then moves on to explore the role and place of the enabling practitioner within these environments. The key thread is the critical importance of the practitioner as the provider of that enabling experience. The chapter then explores, in greater depth, the role of the practitioner as a communicator; highlighting the importance of communication in establishing secure and positive relationships upon which the enabling environment is founded.

Chapter Six builds upon Chapters Three and Four. It incorporates a particular focus on your reflexivity and critical thinking, using a range of contemporary sources to support the development of your critical reflection on practice and your professional development. Reflective practice is offered as a very simple process but one which is sometimes hard to put into effective operation. Some of the reasons and barriers are addressed here, as are some strategies which can aid its realization. This chapter is underpinned with a number of principles, which educators are encouraged to adopt, in support of a belief that relational aspects of work with young children and their families are fundamental to working with them. Furthermore, the chapter argues that space is required for participants to critically share and explore their experiences together.

Chapter Seven focuses on the development of a professional identity for the practitioner. It starts by asking the question, what is a professional? It includes an exploration of the contrasting discourses on professionalism and professional identity, through an introduction of past and current sociological models of professions. It considers critical feminist sociological theories on the construction of an early childhood professional within neo-liberal societies. It explores how feminism challenges traditional discourses on the concept of the professional. It considers the historical and policy background linked to the recent professionalization agenda and current discourses. It asks you to consider and question how the early years' professional is constructed and the part you can play in its construction. You will explore and analyse your own understanding and construction of a professional identity. In conclusion, you are invited to consider research findings in relation to your own emerging professional practice experience, your future employability and opportunities to promote your career development in the early years' workforce.

Chapter Eight considers the role of leadership in early childhood education and care and what it may involve. It identifies models of leadership and the skills and characteristics which support it. It considers the components of teams and team dynamics; it also discusses what makes an effective team and the pressures and constraints that can impact upon effective teamwork. Throughout the chapter you are encouraged to reflect upon your own experiences of being in a team, the roles you tend to adopt and how these impact upon your social and professional interactions with others. It also asks you to consider the role of effective communication in supporting and securing effective teamwork and developing quality leadership skills, particularly in times of change.

References

Oates, R. & Sanders, A. (2008) Making a Little Difference for Early Childhood Studies Students. In T. Papatheodorou & J. Moyles (eds), *Learning Together in the Early Years* (185–195). Abingdon: Routledge.

Papatheodorou, T. & Moyles, J. (2009) (Eds) Learning Together in the Early Years–Exploring Relational Pedagogy. Abingdon: Routledge.

Chapter 1

The student practitioner

Robin Sedgwick

By the end of this chapter you will have an understanding of the following:

- Independent learning.
- The different teaching and learning systems you might encounter at university, and what opportunities they provide.
- Getting the most from university support systems.
- Where to find information and what constitutes a reliable source.
- How to use other people's ideas in your work.
- How to acknowledge your sources.
- What plagiarism is and how to avoid it.
- The different ways you may be required to present information.

Starting university

Whether you are going to university straight from school or college, or re-entering the education system after a break, what you are about to experience will be very different from anything you have previously encountered. The details of your experiences may differ, depending on whether you attend an old university with a depth of tradition or a newer establishment. You might be leaving home to live on your own for the first time or remaining within the family home. You could be studying full-time, enabling you to focus fully on your studies, or perhaps part-time, having to balance your learning with employment and maybe even a family. No matter which combination of these possibilities applies to you, there are certain fundamental challenges you will have to face. The aim of this chapter is to introduce you to strategies to manage some of these challenges and to set you off in the right direction on a very special journey.

Independent learning

If you have ever watched the long-running television quiz show *University Challenge*, you will have seen the student contestants introduce themselves with their name, place of origin and subject. Many will say they are studying a particular subject – English, say, or mathematics. Some however, particularly if they come from one of the older, more traditional universities, will say they are *reading* a subject. Within this simple phrase lies a fundamental truth of the university experience; one does not learn simply by being taught. One learns by taking a proactive stance, reading in depth and exploring the details of your subject.

You will attend classes and lectures as part of your course, but what you gain from them will contribute only a part of your learning experience. If the body of knowledge can be likened to a tree, your tutors will familiarise you with the trunk, or at least part of it. They will probably identify the various branches and where they start, maybe even venturing some way along one or two of them. But that is as far as they can take you. It is up to you to continue the exploration of the branches towards the detail of the twigs and leaves. To do this successfully, you must be able to take control of your study and develop the ability to follow up the ideas and themes your tutors introduce to you. You must become an *independent learner*.

Teaching and learning at university

One of the big changes that you will experience when you start higher education, particularly if you have just come from a traditional school or college background, is in the nature of the teaching and learning experience. This may be very different to the classroom-based sessions you have previously enjoyed. The three sessions you are likely to meet are the lecture, the seminar and the tutorial.

Lectures

The word lecture comes from the Latin word *lectura*, meaning reading. Generally your lectures will be arranged at a programme or faculty level and you will be provided with a timetable of lectures. If there is such a thing as a 'traditional style of lecture', it would probably be an hour session in which 100 or more students sit in a tiered lecture theatre taking notes, while listening to the discourse of the lecturer. While this situation does still exist in reality, lectures can take many formats, and even two lectures in ostensibly the same format may be different due to variations in lecturer style.

What generally will hold true, however, is that the lecture will be delivered by someone who is a subject specialist. What a lecture will not do, though, is provide a full coverage of a topic. It will set out some key ideas, and perhaps introduce you to some important writers in the field; it may even pose questions for you to consider. To return to the tree of knowledge analogy, the lecture will identify part of the trunk and indicate the start of a particular branch. It is then up to you to follow up the session, and for this purpose most lectures will provide a set of references and suggestions for follow-up reading. Also there usually will be a list of recommended books for that particular course or module. You will probably need to take notes during the session, although often notes may be available through an online virtual learning environment (VLE). Depending on the lecturer's preference and style, these may be accessed before the session to provide a framework to be built on, or after the session to summarise the ideas covered.

The format of a lecture will be determined by the preferences of the tutor and the size of the group. Where there are more than, say, 30 students present the session is more likely to resemble the traditional one outlined earlier, with students playing a passive role and experiencing little, if any, interaction with the lecturer. However, with smaller groups, students may take a more active role with the lecturer asking questions or eliciting ideas from the students. In sessions like this the distinguishing line between a lecture and a seminar can become blurred. Lectures may involve several approaches within the course of one session; there may be activities where one works with a partner or within a small group, or perhaps the lecture may be a split session commencing with a traditional delivery to a large group, which then divides into smaller seminar groups. Inevitably you will experience a wide variety of lecture types as different lecturers, even within the same subject area, will have different styles and approaches.

Top tips: How to get the most out of lectures

- Attend all timetabled lectures. Often a lecture will build on a foundation of knowledge from a previous session. If you missed that session you will struggle to understand the current one.
- If you have an idea what the lecture is going to be on, perhaps from the lecturer's scheme of work, do some background reading on the key ideas.
- Ensure that you carry out any pre-lecture preparation that is required.
- If notes are available on a VLE before the session, make sure you print them off, or download to a tablet, and take them with you. During the lecture you can supplement them with additional information.
- Listen carefully during the lecture and try to identify the key points. Your note-taking strategy should not distract you from what is being said.
- Read through your notes as soon as you can after the session to ensure they make sense. Seek clarification on any points you do not understand.
- Follow up references and suggested follow up reading.
- Discuss the lecture with your fellow students. They may have grasped key points that you missed, or perhaps they interpreted what they heard in a different way.

Seminars

A seminar is a group discussion. The word is derived from the Latin word *seminarium*, meaning 'seed plot'. The seeds to be sown are the seeds of ideas.

A seminar will usually be focused on a particular topic and may be arranged after a lecture to discuss the issues raised by it. On other occasions there may be a need for personal preparation, in which students familiarize themselves with an area of theory – perhaps a book chapter, academic paper or area of policy which will be the focus of the discussion. The leader of the seminar will most likely be the course tutor, although student-led seminars are possible. Just as there are different styles of lectures, so seminars may differ. In some the seminar leader may actively seek to involve all the individual members of the group. In others, he or she could let the discussion flow freely, with individuals making contributions as they see fit.

Another possibility is that individuals may be required to give a presentation to the rest of the group. This could be centred on topics allocated in advance by the tutor or might be something personal, such as a description about their ideas for a research topic. The presentation could be a simple verbal description or might be focused on something like an academic poster. It might involve using visual aids such as PowerPoint and could be delivered by either an individual or a group. This type of presentation may be used as a learning device to encourage analysis of a particular area or, in some cases, even be used as an assessment component.

Top tips: How to get the most out of seminars

- Ensure that you do any required preparation before the session. Read set texts and identify their key points. Use these to formulate questions you can ask during the session.
- If you are expected to give a presentation, remember the keys to success are the four Ps: plan, prepare, practise, present. See the section later in this chapter on how to deliver an effective PowerPoint presentation.
- Reflect on the content after the session.

Tutorials

The tutorial is historically a fundamental part of the British university system in which students, either individually or in small groups, meet with their tutor. Tutorials exist for a variety of purposes: to assist students encountering difficulties, to provide formative feedback on work in progress or simply to provide a forum for discussion of key issues.

The number of students in a tutorial will vary from institution to institution. In some universities one to one tutorials may not be available and group tutorials may be the norm, in which case you may find the session becomes much closer to a seminar. However, as a student of early childhood studies, it is most likely that you will have a personal tutor whose role it is to oversee your practice in work placement. Your tutor may be someone who lectures to you, or it may be another member of the teaching team. One practice you may encounter is where a small number of starter lectures are delivered to a group, after which each student is allocated a tutor to support further progress. This is often the system used when you are engaged in a research project such as a final-year dissertation. Tutorials may be timetabled at regular times or you may have to book a time slot, either by signing up to a list or by emailing the tutor. There may be no compulsion to do this, and many students do not take up their tutorial opportunities, despite the fact there is a strong correlation between tutorial attendance and good grades. Tutorials are capable of adding a high degree of clarity to your learning, particularly in helping you to determine what exactly is required from an essay or other assignment.

Top tips: How to get the most out of tutorials

- Take all tutorial opportunities.
- Make a note of dates and times in your diary. Ensure you know where the tutorial will be held and you can find your way there.
- Be on time. There may be other students booked in for tutorials, and your tutor may have allocated specific time slots.
- Ensure you have completed any preparation that is needed.
- Don't be afraid to ask questions. One of the express functions of a tutorial is to give you the opportunity to do just that. Part of your preparation for the tutorial should be to decide on the questions you will ask.

Getting the most from university

As you navigate your way through university life, you do not need to do so on your own. Advice, support and information will be available from a variety of sources. You should expect most of the following to be available, although the specific name of each may vary from university to university.

- Programme leader
- Year or stage tutor
- Academic tutors
- Personal tutor
- Subject specific library support
- Learning support
- Peer mentoring
- Careers advisory service
- Student welfare officers
- Disability support
- IT technical support
- IT skills support
- Student health services
- Student counselling services
- Student's union
- Faith services
- Security services.

If any problems arise, your first point of contact may be your course leader, year tutor or personal tutor. Even if they cannot directly provide support, they will know the university systems well enough to point you in the direction of where it can be found. Experience has shown that personal problems frequently impact on study, and a supportive tutor who is aware of your situation may be able to arrange extra tutorial time, provide extensions on assignment submission dates and be prepared to argue your case at assessment boards.

The range of support on offer may be extensive, but is of no use if you do not access it in times of need. Your pride may be a barrier to you accessing support, but often the most successful students are those who are able to identify the occasions when support or guidance is needed.

Finding information

As previously outlined, much of the study at university is independent learning and requires you to find information – either material which has been specifically identified on reading lists, or material you need to gather together to investigate a particular topic. Your two most likely starting points will be the university library and online. Increasingly these two sources are becoming one, as the twenty-first century university library, as well as holding a stock of books and other academic publications, acts as a gateway to an enormous range of online resources.

The library

At first encounter the university library can be overwhelming. As it is going to be so important in your life, it is important that you uncover its secrets as quickly as possible.

- There should be library tours available for new students, either by booking through the library, or provided by your programme of study as part of your induction programme. If these are delivered by an early childhood studies subject-specialist librarian, all the better!
- Check what information is available, either as printed leaflets or online guides. These may be prepared on a subject-specific basis, outlining the availability of resources on specific topics.
- You will need answers to the following:
  o How many books can I have out at any one time?
  o How long can I borrow a book for? This may vary from text to text, with particularly popular texts having a short loan time. Where multiple copies of a text are available some might be available on a long loan and others on a short one. There may also be reference copies which remain in the library.
  o How do I renew a book?
  o What are the fines if a book is overdue? These can be punitive, particularly on popular short loan texts, but can be avoided if you maintain an accurate record of due dates.
- Take some time to explore the library at leisure and find where the books you need are situated. Books will be arranged according to a numerical classification

system called the *Dewey Decimal System*. If you are not familiar with this you can look it up online. Unfortunately there is no single section for early childhood studies and material is spread throughout the library at numbers which reflect the different aspects of the subject:

o   Nursery Nursing at 649.1
o   Child Welfare at 362.7
o   Child Development at 155.4
o   Sociology at 306.87.

To locate a particular topic use a keyword search in the library catalogue. This will be available at terminals within the library and will usually also be available online so it can be accessed off campus.

Library resources and facilities

Most university libraries will have the following:

- Books
- Periodicals and academic journals
- Video and DVD recordings
- An electronic library catalogue
- Computer work stations
- Silent study areas
- Group study areas
- Printers
- Photocopiers
- Specialist collections – for example, children's books and resources for use on work placement.

If your library has a subject-specialist librarian for early childhood studies, ensure you make full use of him or her. They are experts in their field, and a quick email asking where particular information might be found can often save hours of frustration.

The electronic library

This is the gateway to a huge range of resources and may be accessed on or off campus, either directly or through the university website. Typically it will allow you to access the following.

- Library catalogue
- Electronic journals
- Databases

- Library guides and tutorials
- Copyright-free image and multimedia collections
- Exam papers
- Online newspapers
- Electronic books
- Online help and support from a librarian.

There may also be a subject-specific area that lists journals, electronic books and websites that are relevant to early childhood. During the first year of study you probably will be most reliant on books as sources of information. As you progress, however, you will be expected to make use of journal articles. Academic journals publish original research and provide the ultimate source of much of what goes into textbooks.

University electronic resources

When you become a member of a university you gain access to a wide range of electronic resources. The university library has already been mentioned, but in addition, logging on (which will require a username and password) will enable you to access some, or all, of the following.

- Timetables
- Career development
- A personal university email account
- IT support
- Course and tutor details
- Your personal details – module choices and, eventually, grades
- An area on the university IT network to store files
- A virtual learning environment (VLE)
- Areas to electronically submit work.

If you are not well-conversant with information technology, then you will need to make a conscious effort to come to grips with the university IT systems as they provide essential channels of communication, information and resourcing. You may be introduced to the systems as part of an induction or library tour or you may need to pick up, or download, a guide to help you navigate the systems. If you are struggling, support sessions may be available; check with the library staff – they are there to help you.

Virtual learning environment

E-learning is a term that covers a range of online methods used for presenting a range of materials and resources for learning. Most universities deliver these using a web-based virtual learning environment (VLE), such as Blackboard, WebCT or Moodle.

A VLE can usually be accessed off campus, and perhaps even on a smartphone once you have installed the appropriate application, and will provide a range of tools. Typically there will be an online area for each of your courses or modules. Within these you will probably find a selection of the following:

- Course and module handbooks
- Specifications and schemes of work
- *Communication* channels and contact details
- Course *news and announcements*
- *Resources* and *materials* to download or view
- Copies of lecture notes, PowerPoint presentations and recordings (audio or video) of lectures
- Assignment guidelines
- Old exam papers
- Interactive features such as wikis, blogs and discussion groups
- Facilities for the submission of written work.

You should get into the habit of checking your university email account and visiting the VLE every day, to pick up any announcements or messages. These may appear on the home page of the VLE to alert you of cancelled classes, late timetable changes or approaching deadlines. The VLE will usually link to email so that announcements will be sent directly to you as well.

Reliability of sources

The reliability of a source relates to the extent to which it can be trusted.

We live in an information age characterised by instant access to the World Wide Web and the vast storehouse of information it provides. One of the issues that new students often struggle with is what constitutes a reliable source of information.

With the ability of any individual or organization to place material on the Web it has become increasingly difficult to be certain as to the reliability of sources, and the ability of a student to evaluate the reliability of information found online has become an essential skill. You will need to assess whether data are reliable and whether information is fact or opinion. In order to appreciate what constitutes a reliable source we need to consider how knowledge originates and is disseminated.

New knowledge is gained through research and scholarship, and the ideas within it are communicated by publication in an academic journal. An academic journal is a periodical whose purpose is to provide a forum for the publication, discussion and critique of new work. Journals are published at regular intervals and are available through subscriptions held by individuals and institutions such as universities. They can be accessed through the university library, either as a paper copy or, more likely, in electronic format. Research published in academic journals is often reported by the popular news media; some of the journals you may have heard of in news reports are the *British Medical Journal*, *The Lancet* (a medical journal) and the science journal

Nature. Within the field of early childhood studies there are journals with titles such as *Early Child Development and Care*, the *Journal of Child and Family Studies* and *Children's Health Care*. As can be seen from the titles, journals frequently have a very narrow area of interest. Articles that appear in journals are peer reviewed – they have been scrutinised by other scholars in the field to determine that the content is of sufficiently high quality and originality to merit publication. It is this process of peer review that makes journal articles stand out as a reliable source. Some original ideas may also be published in books and may not be peer reviewed. The material that is published in journals and original books forms the basis of knowledge that is then incorporated into secondary sources such as books, magazine articles, newspaper articles and websites. It is in dealing with these secondary sources that the student must be critical and selective in the choice of information. As ideas and information are incorporated into secondary sources, they are frequently adapted, rephrased or simplified and meanings may change. This is often unintentional, but in some cases may be deliberate, an author perhaps giving only one side of an argument or being selective with the facts. This is particularly the case with newspaper articles, which may often seek to represent the political position of the newspaper's owners.

At the start of your university career you will almost certainly be relying on secondary sources, mainly the academic textbooks in the university library. As you progress, however, your tutors will expect you more and more to go to the original sources of information and will expect you to access journal articles.

So, on what criteria are you expected to make your critical selection of information? The original sources are usually safe to use, although it is important to be aware of the distinction between fact and opinion. In the study of childhood there are many areas in which processes are taking place which cannot be directly observed. How children learn and how they develop emotionally are two examples of fields of study where researchers have put forward explanations for what is happening. Sometimes these explanations can be in conflict with each other, and an area becomes *contested*. As a student of childhood, it is important to appreciate that in many areas there are no empirical truths and no right or wrong answers.

In evaluating secondary sources there are a number of questions that you can ask:

- Do you know who wrote it? Who do they work for?
- Is it based on identified original sources?
- Is it recent? Old is not necessarily bad. An old piece of work that has been highly influential can still be important, but ideas change over the years.
- Can you cross-reference, and find the same information in another source?
- Is it clear whether the information is fact or opinion?
- Is the information presented by an individual or organization that might stand to gain from promoting particular ideas? This is particularly important when evaluating websites.
- Can the information be used to generalise outside the context in which it originally appears?

Books

You will be provided with a reading list for your course and for each component module, and the question of whether to buy books will arise. In deciding whether to purchase, you need to consider how much you will use a particular book. There may well be some key texts that will form the core of a section of study that you will need to refer to regularly, and these might be a worthwhile purchase. In following up your reading list, is important that you check what the library contains. Texts recommended by lecturers will usually be held in stock, but may be difficult to obtain at times when demand is high. A third alternative is to access an e-book. University libraries hold electronic copies of some popular texts, which can be accessed online, either on or off campus. Usually there is an option to either read the book online or download it for a limited period. For copyright reasons there are limits on copying or printing the text. Some will allow the printing of a small number of pages, and others will allow no printing at all. To find the location of a particular book or to search for books on a particular topic, you will need to access the library catalogue. This will usually be available online off campus, and will enable you to source books through a keyword or author search. It will identify how many copies of each book are available and where they are held. If books are out on loan it may even tell you when they are due back. Additionally it will enable you to check details of your library account, such as loans, renewal dates and (hopefully not!) fines. It will probably allow you to renew texts online so long as the book has not been reserved by another borrower and, if all copies are on loan, enable you to reserve one when it is returned. If you find that your library does not hold a particular book, it can be borrowed from another library as an interlibrary loan, although you may be charged for this.

When selecting a book to use, it is important that it is of the correct academic level. If you have come to your early childhood studies degree having previously studied a CACHE or BTEC diploma at level 3, the texts you will have relied on there will be inappropriate for use in a degree programme at levels 4, 5 and 6.

Journals

The latest editions of key journals may well be on display for easy access. Older editions will be archived on shelves or in movable stacks. Increasingly, journal articles are accessed online, using the university library as a gateway. Keyword searches will enable articles on particular topics to be identified, or you can browse electronically through the back issues of a particular journal. University libraries will subscribe to a number of different electronic providers, and you may find that an article is available from more than one supplier. If you encounter any problems accessing any electronic resources you should contact a librarian for assistance. There are usually no restrictions on downloading a copy of a journal article. However, it is important to realize that most companies that provide online journals do so on a commercial basis. Your university pays subscriptions so that you are entitled to access them free of charge, but they then must be accessed through the university's online pathways. If you try to access journal articles by any other means, perhaps having been directed to a publisher's website by a search engine, you may well find that articles are available only on a pay-to-view basis.

The university digital library will list the journal titles available, enabling you to find a particular article if you have a full reference for it. If you are looking for journal articles on a particular topic, there are search platforms from which electronic journals can be accessed; EBSCO and the British Education Index are probably the two most useful. On these you can perform a keyword search, or perhaps you might browse past editions of a journal whose area of interest is specific to your field of enquiry.

The World Wide Web

In December 2012 there were an estimated 634 million websites with 51 million having been added in the previous 12 months. That number will now be considerably larger. Most people when searching online will simply pop what they seek into a search engine. This process has become so ubiquitous that *google* is now included in online dictionaries as a verb! It is very tempting to search for information in this way, but, convenient as it may seem, it is unlikely to provide the quality of information required. Your lecturers will tell you that you need to be sourcing information from reliable academic sources. Academic sources can be regarded as those with peer reviewed content (mainly journal articles) and those which are compiled from those sources (mainly academic textbooks). Unfortunately most search engine hits fall into neither category, and even though they may locate quality academic material, it may not be readily accessible, as we have already seen. That is not to say that reliable information does not exist on the Web. It is there, but you need to be able to discriminate between those sources which are academically reliable and those which are not. Some of the criteria you can consider in evaluating the reliability of a source are as follows.

- The author: If an author is not listed, in most cases you should disregard the source. If an author is named you may try investigating his or her credentials to see if he or she is published, appears in a scholarly journal or is employed by a research institute or university.
- The URL: This is the website address, and it tells you about the nature of the hosting organization. A *.ac* ending indicates a UK academic organization, and *.edu* indicates one outside the UK. The information on such a site will usually be reliable, but one should be aware that a page may consist of opinion rather than fact, with no named author and possibly an element of bias.

  If the site ends in *.gov* it is a government website and usually a reliable source of statistics, legislation, policy documents and reports. These sites can be invaluable as they provide up-to-date material online years before it will find its way into a textbook.

  The domains *.co* and *.com* indicate sites which exist for commercial purposes. If you put 'child development' into a search engine you will come up with a plethora of sites, many of which are .co or .com sites and directed at parents. They may be sponsored by magazines or companies that wish to sell child-oriented products, although it often can be difficult to identify who actually runs the site. Generally popular sites such as these should be avoided, as the academic standard of information they provide is usually not commensurate with that required for a degree programme.

The domain *.org* is a tricky one. It was originally intended for use by non-profit organizations, although it is now used by commercial organizations. Nevertheless there are many excellent resources to be found on .org sites. Many charities and research foundations exist in this domain, two excellent examples being the websites of the *Joseph Rowntree Foundation* and the *Child Poverty Action Group*. These are both organizations with an agenda focused on poverty and deprivation in the UK, who sponsor reports that include independent research findings. You must nevertheless tread carefully as some *.org* sites may be hosted by advocacy groups or pressure groups which adhere to a particular political or social perspective. While they may contain reliable information, you need to be aware that there could be a strong element of bias.

- Online journals and magazines: A general rule of thumb here is to look at the end of the article. Is there a list of references that relate to scholarly non-Internet sources? If so, the article is probably reputable.

    o News sites: It is very tempting to use online mass media sites, but they are generally reporting on something which has been published elsewhere, may be written by a non-expert and, particularly in the case of newspaper sites, may have a strong element of bias. Ideally, you need to track down the original source. Where the news site can prove useful, though, is in indicating where the source of the original information can be found. The BBC news site is particularly good at identifying sources, often providing a hyperlink to the original report or journal article.

Presenting information

Written university assignments come in many different forms. Some examples are essays, reports, case studies and dissertations. All of these will test your skills in finding and analysing information and will require you to demonstrate your knowledge and understanding of a topic by putting forward your ideas in a fluent academic style of writing.

Using others' ideas in your work

An aspect of written assignments that may come as a surprise is that your personal opinions on a particular topic are not necessarily required. Through your extensive reading you will be exposed to the ideas, theories, knowledge and opinions of notable researchers authors and academics, and it is these that you should be using in your work. Unless you are involved in a study that requires you to engage in primary research, there is no expectation that you should be creating new knowledge. What you should be doing is using the knowledge that is already in existence to construct your arguments and discussion. Of course, you must not pass the ideas of others off as your own. To do so constitutes *plagiarism*, which is a serious academic offence.

Plagiarism: what forms it takes and how to avoid it

Its basic meaning, according to the Oxford Dictionary, is 'the practice of taking someone else's work or ideas and passing them off as one's own'. It comes from the Latin word *plagiarius*, meaning 'kidnapper'.

The University of Derby online plagiarism tutorial PLATO (University of Derby 2012) identifies three forms of plagiarism: collusion, copying and paraphrasing.

Collusion is working secretly with another person, or in a group, to produce work which should have been just your own work. It should not be confused with the legitimate practice of cooperation, in which there is no attention to deceive or gain marks unfairly.

Copying is to reproduce a passage using identical or very similar words. A copy could be made from a book, a journal article or the work of another student, and, crucially, you attempt to pass off the copy as your own work. If, however, you acknowledge the copy in your work by placing it in quotation marks and identifying the source by means of a reference, it becomes legitimate practice.

Paraphrasing is similar to copying, in that you take somebody else's ideas and attempt to pass them off as your own, in this case by rephrasing the ideas in your own words. At first this may appear legitimate, but on reflection it is clear that you have stolen another's intellectual property. Just as with copying, the source of the ideas must be acknowledged through referencing, although if you have paraphrased, there is no requirement to use quotation marks.

Referencing: the conventions of referencing

So how does one avoid the pitfalls of plagiarism and acknowledge when you have copied or paraphrased another's ideas? The answer, of course, is to *reference*.

Referencing has to fulfil two purposes. Firstly it has to indicate to the reader that, at a particular part of the text, the ideas are those of someone other than the writer. Secondly the referencing has to enable the reader to easily find the source of those ideas. There are several ways to do this, but the one you are most likely to encounter is the Harvard system, and that is the one briefly outlined here. There are several interpretations of the Harvard system, but the preferred system will be indicated in your course handbook and promoted by your lecturers and tutors; it is important that you become familiar with its various conventions.

The Harvard system consists of two parts: a citation in the text and a full reference that appears in a list of references at the end of the work. The citation consists of the author's surname and year of publication. This may be incorporated into the structure of the sentence, or stand alone after the idea to which it relates – for example:

Smith (1983) describes how toddlers are interested in other children of their own age.

Toddlers are interested in other children of their own age (Smith 1983).

Where there are two authors, both are listed. If three or more are listed, the Latin phrase *et al.* (short for *et alia*, meaning *and others*) can be used – for example, a work by Smith, Jones and Williams (2009) would be cited as Smith *et al.* (2009).

These citations in the text will each link to a full reference contained in a list of references, arranged in alphabetical order by author surname, at the end of the piece. The information to identify each source is presented in a prescribed order. For a book this is as follows:

Author surname, Author initial. (Year of publication). Title. Edition (if not the first). Place of publication. Publisher.

Thus a full reference would appear as follows:

> Rowling, J.K. (2000). *Harry Potter and the Goblet of Fire*. London. Bloomsbury Press.

For a journal article there is a similar set order:

> Author surname, author initial. (year of publication). Title of article. Name of journal. Volume. Part number. Pages.

This would give us the following:

> Plowman, L., Stephen, C. and McPake, J. (2010). Supporting young children's learning with technology at home and in preschool. *Research Papers in Education*, 25: 1, 93–113.

Note that the three authors are listed in full. You can use *et al.* in the citation but not in the full reference. Hence the citation in the text would be Plowman *et al.* (2010).

And for an Internet source, the format is as follows:

> Author surname, author initial. (year of publication) Title of article / webpage. [Internet] Available at: full URL. Date accessed: day-month-year.

Here is an example:

> BBC News. (2010) Gruffalo tops list of children's favourite books. [Internet] Available at: www.bbc.co.uk/news/education-11568551. Date accessed: 22-10-2013.

Note in the last example that where no author is given, the first part of the reference is the name of the organization hosting the site. This will also appear in the citation. Note also that the *full* URL of the page is given, not just that of the website home page. The reference should enable the reader to go directly to the source.

The list of references is not the same as a bibliography. The list of references includes only the sources that have been cited in the text, whereas a bibliography will include all sources you have consulted. An assignment brief will usually indicate which of these is required.

Plagiarism detection software

In many universities electronic submission of written work has become the norm, enabling the use of plagiarism detection software, the most commonly used being *Turnitin*. This is an online service which matches the student's submitted text against an extensive library of Internet pages, journals, periodicals and previously submitted student essays. Staff and students can access an *originality report*, which indicates the percentage of text matched – that is, the percentage that is thought to have been copied, as well as the suspected sources. This serves two purposes: it enables students to spot text which is not their own words and therefore should be referenced. Secondly, it catches the tiny minority of students who attempt to cheat by constructing assignments from unacknowledged sources cut and pasted from the Web. To use a motoring analogy, *Turnitin* serves as both a speedometer to enable compliance with the law and a speed camera to identify those who break it.

How to present information: essays, reports and presentations

Essays

The word essay comes from the Latin *exigere*, meaning to examine or test. The essay is a traditional form of university assessment and one that has a clearly defined form and structure. It is a piece of prose, written in the third person, which closely examines a particular topic. It is structured as a series of paragraphs and the use of bullet points, side headings and diagrams is not considered appropriate. Burns and Sinfield (2008) use what they call the *legal precedent model* to describe and explain the structure of an essay. This likens the essay writer to a barrister in court defending a client. The barrister must convince a jury of his or her client's innocence, and the essay writer must convince a reader as to the validity of the case he or she is making. At the start of the trial the barrister sets out what line the defence will take, what he or she will attempt to prove to the jury and what conclusion they should reach. In a similar way an essay should have an introductory paragraph that sets out what ideas and arguments will be used and what conclusion will be reached. It is this latter point that new students often struggle to grasp, but it is important to remember that an academic essay is not a crime thriller in which the identity of the murderer is withheld until the final scene. If TV's *Midsomer Murders* or *CSI* were presented in the style of an academic essay, we would be told in the first five minutes who the suspects were and which one was the perpetrator! However, the shows might diminish in popularity.

To return to the legal analogy, to convince the jury our barrister must prove the accused's innocence by providing evidence. This will involve calling witnesses and perhaps specialists in fields such as forensics. You, the essay writer, will similarly provide evidence by calling on witnesses and specialists; in this case they will be the authors you have encountered in your reading. This is where you will be using other people's ideas to construct your debate and argument, not forgetting, of course, to reference your sources appropriately.

Finally we come to the conclusion. The barrister will remind the jury of the reasons why they should find the accused not guilty and remind them of the evidence that supports that conclusion. You, the writer, should remind the reader of the main points that you have made and what conclusion they point to. It may well be, if the subject of the essay is in a contested area, that you have to weigh up points for and against before deciding where the balance lies.

The essay therefore consists of three parts. To summarise in a simpler and easily remembered form, there is an old maxim:

In the introduction you tell 'em what you are going to tell 'em.
In the main body you tell 'em.
In the conclusion you remind 'em what you told 'em.

Reports

Whereas an essay is characterised by a formal structure and a limitation as to what can be included, a report has no such restrictions. Material can be arranged under side headings or as bullet points or presented in flow charts, tables or diagrams. A particular example of when you might be asked to produce a report is as part of a work placement or practice module. Observations are fundamental in understanding and monitoring children's development, and as part of an early years work placement you will almost certainly be expected to observe some aspect of a child's development and then write up the results. In this you will probably evaluate what you have discovered about the child's level of development and relate your findings to the Early Years Foundation Stage (DfE 2012) and the accepted developmental norms. You may also evaluate your own performance in terms of how well you managed the observational techniques employed.

Presentations

Presentations may involve talking about a particular topic for a specified period of time. You may be supported by a poster you have produced or you could be using presentation software such as PowerPoint. Either of these will involve an oral presentation to an audience, usually a group of fellow students, and is best approached using a technique already mentioned – the four Ps.

Plan
Prepare
Practise
Present

Giving an oral presentation is, for many students, one of the most worrying things they have to do. Invariably you will be very nervous, but experience has shown that it is an area where practice pays off.

Top tips: PowerPoint

Having sat through numerous student presentations, the author suggests the following tips to address the commonest errors and weaknesses:

- Choose a slide design which is visually appealing, but not distracting or cluttered.
- Choose a font colour that contrasts strongly with the background. What might look fine on your computer screen might be hard to read when projected in a lighted room.
- Include relevant images in some of your slides to increase visual interest.
- Do not put too many words on a slide.
- If using bullet points, consider using the animation feature to reveal your points one by one.

- The more spectacular slide transition and animation styles should be used sparingly as they can distract from content.
- When presenting, do not just read from the slides. What you should be aiming for is to have key points on the slides that you can then talk about in an 'off the cuff' fashion. This is not easy to achieve, however, and requires practice and a confidence in your delivery and subject knowledge that comes only with experience. It is something you will need to work on. Perhaps you might start by using this technique on just one slide in a presentation.
- Engage with your audience. Make eye contact. Do not become fixed on your notes or the screen. This becomes much easier when you have mastered the technique described in the previous point.
- Don't talk too quickly. Use a range of vocal inflexions rather than a monotone drone.
- Try to enjoy the experience.

Conclusion

This brief chapter has hopefully whetted your appetite for university study. It has identified a number of important areas that you will need to come to grips with as soon as possible, if you are to make the most of what the university has to offer you. You will undoubtedly find that there are skills that you need to develop or areas of weakness you need to strengthen. A trip to the university library will enable you to access a host of volumes that will enable you to develop your study skills, improve your academic writing and maximise your chances of success. Your lecturers, tutors and university support systems are there to help you, as are your peers – your fellow students whose friendship and support can make a vital contribution to achieving your goal. Enjoy your academic journey; your period of study should provide not only the knowledge, skills and qualification that underpin your future career but also an experience that can be fondly remembered in the years to come.

References

Burns, T. and Sinfield, S. (2008). *Essential Study Skills*. London: SAGE.

DfE. (2012). *Statutory Framework for the Early Years Foundation Stage* (Internet). Available at: www.foundationyears.org.uk/early-years-foundation-stage-2012/. Date accessed: 25-7-2013.

University of Derby. (2012). *PLATO – PLAgiarism Teaching Online* (Internet). Available at: https://plato.derby.ac.uk/plagiarism1/types.html. Date accessed: 4-6-2013.

Chapter 2

The student as researcher

Jon White with Christine Hey and Ruby Oates

By the end of this chapter you will:

- Have understood what research is and reasons for doing it.
- Have addressed the ethical issues raised by research.
- Know what makes a good literature review.
- Considered some research methodologies.
- Explored some strategies for carrying out research.
- Understand what you can do with your research.

Introduction

What is research?

Anyone who has spent time in an early years' setting will know that there is debate over the question of what is high-quality provision and practice. There may be disagreement between practitioners over what *best practice* is, as well as difficulties associated with communicating the reasons for doing things in a particular way to the parents of the children in the setting (Sylva & Taylor 2006).

Perhaps in the past, it has been acceptable for the practice in settings to be *anecdote-driven* – things done in a particular way because that is how it has always been done. However, the increasing demands for high-quality provision have led to the development of practice which is *evidence-led*. This means that it is based on what has been uncovered through research, and practitioners are in a much stronger position to explain and justify their professional decisions, both to each other and to the parents of the children they care for. Practitioners find themselves asking questions about what happens in their setting. This is what is meant by research.

In some places, a researcher may be seen as someone surrounded by books, working in a quiet place and doing a lot of hard thinking.

Or, a researcher may be a practitioner surrounded by children, working in a noisy place and doing a lot of observing and reflecting.

Of course, both are types of research, but it is likely that if you are studying early childhood studies in higher education, you are going to find yourself in both groups, most likely undertaking *action research*. This means that your research will be undertaken in practice and anything you find out will apply to practice.

This research *into* practice happens *in* practice, and has contributed to early childhood studies being recognised as an influential academic discipline. There are now subject-specific journals and a large number of books devoted to early childhood, with a substantial population of early childhood studies graduates in the workforce; this indicates the importance of early childhood studies as a subject in its own right, exerting national and international influence. As reflective practitioners, we need to recognise that the world shifts and we need to shift with it, maintaining practice which is truly fit for its purpose (Dahlberg 2007). We should be confident to ask questions about the work we do and its impact on children. For example, Dahlberg (2007) questions the purpose of the early childhood institution and asks serious questions about how early years' stakeholders see the places in which they work – whether they see the setting as a business, a factory or as an agent of cultural reproduction.

Activity

Take a moment to think about your experience in your placement.

Do you recognise any of Dahlberg's descriptions in relation to your placement or early years' work setting?

Discuss, in groups, observing appropriate ethical practice, what leads you to these conclusions.

Dahlberg (2007) also asks questions about the role of early years' practitioners; do they see themselves as technicians (working with objective processes to achieve identifiable outcomes), as substitute parents (a nurturing role) or as entrepreneurs (running a business)?

Oates, in Chapter Seven, explores these potential identities in greater detail. As a researcher, therefore, there are opportunities to explore how children and adults *feel* (subjectively) about different aspects of their lives as well as the *measured* impact that adult decisions have on the children in their care. Both can be valid and reliable approaches to research.

What does research look like?

This section continues with a discussion of the two basic research *approaches* which the student researcher will face. These are quite different ways of thinking; they are called *research paradigms*. While each paradigm has its supporters, the approach taken to research may be seen to underpin something more fundamental in the beliefs of the researcher regarding their attitude towards children and their development.

The first method is where the researcher takes a 'modernist' or 'positivist' approach. This might include a methodology which focuses on measuring in an objective, scientific way to collect information. This usually tends to separate the researcher from the participants and aims to make the research more formal. It may try to reduce the question being asked to one single factor and then measure the impact of varying this.

Typically, this approach will include questionnaires and interviews with closed questions, timed observations and content analysis. The modernist researcher may look for a correlation (connection) between the factors which are being investigated. This approach may also include any research methodology in which numerical data is gathered.

The student researcher will need to reflect on whether it is appropriate to take such a reductionist approach when researching aspects of childhood. This would mean a focus on one narrow area of interest, to the exclusion of all else; this reduces the behaviour and abilities of a child to a single factor. Is the scientific method, which characterises these strategies, likely to provide information which is both reliable and valid? Can you really isolate one single factor to investigate, ignoring all other parts of the life of your participants?

The modernist approach is contrasted with a postmodern approach, in which children, their community and notions of childhood are seen in a holistic way; this is also known as interpretivism (for more, see Denzin & Lincoln 2005). The issues investigated may involve conducting research in the child's environment – for example, an early years' setting, where the researcher is either directly involved in activities, or indirectly involved through the use of journals or diaries. Increasing use is made of group discussions and meta-analysis, where the researcher has to distil themes and interpret meanings. Mac Naughton (2005) describes this as rhizo-analysis, essentially a strategy for trying to understand how the child sees the world and makes meaning and connections between the network of people and events in his or her world. In contrast to a modernist scientific approach, where the outcomes are measured, this interpretivist approach may be more open to a range of interpretations.

However, while the interpretivist approach may be able to provide detailed insights into behaviour, it is notoriously difficult to interpret findings and to reach any kind of certainty regarding what is learned from the research. Student researchers may find themselves overwhelmed with information of different types, and so they have to be very selective in how the material is managed.

There is much to commend those researchers who manage to combine these two approaches, making objective judgements where appropriate, while at the same time ensuring that there is always time to explore the unexpected thoughts and feelings of their participants; this is often referred to as a mixed methods approach. An ability to bring these together provides strong support for any conclusions drawn or recommendations made. This may be considered to be a way of raising the quality or rigour of the research. As you explore this concept more fully, you will find that postmodernists consider that there may actually be no single answer to a question, as all research findings are vulnerable to the research values, circumstances or context in which the research was undertaken (for more, see Mac Naughton & Hughes 2009).

Ethics and research

When carrying out investigations, it is a professional responsibility for the student researcher to behave appropriately. This is why a set of principles called ethical guidelines have been established and need to be followed; this section introduces the issues associated with the *conduct and behaviour* of the student as researcher. It is particularly important that these guidelines are followed when working with children, as they are not in a legal position to provide consent. It is easy to find examples in research where children have been taken advantage of.

Consider two cases where children have been used in research.

1. Watson and Rayner (1920) used a boy called little Albert in conditioning experiments, teaching him to associate a white rat (which he liked) with a loud noise (which frightened him). Was it ethical to try to learn about learning by making a little boy cry?
2. Genie was a girl who had been kept in isolation. She was then studied by researchers interested in language development. Was it ethical to study Genie in this way? (Curtiss 1977)

No one is suggesting that any student researcher would behave like this now, but it is important to recognise that children are especially vulnerable to pressure from researchers due to their acceptance of the norm of doing as they are told (Coady 2010).

Researchers will, however, need to justify the work they do. One of the ways in which the cost or time incurred in doing research can be justified is by saying that it brings benefits to a large number of people. Watson and Rayner (1920) argued that it is important to try to maximise learning, so that children can perform better at school and into their adult lives. Anything which contributes to a better understanding of learning is justified – including making the boy cry. Do you agree?

Consider

A student is interested in the way children learn about sharing. To explore this, the student sets up a game for the children where there is not enough equipment to go round. This leads to an argument, and several children are upset because they are excluded.

Afterwards, the student explains the reasons for this activity and what she had hoped they would learn from it.

Do you feel comfortable that the upset caused was worth it?

There are a variety of research guidelines to follow. These are set by the institutions caring for the children involved, the authority supervising the student conducting the research and the relevant professional associations. Accessible guidelines are published by:

- The European Early Childhood Education Research Association
- The British Educational Research Association
- The British Psychological Society
- The British Sociological Association.

Sedgwick, in Chapter One, provides further advice regarding ethical policies in individual higher education institutions.

Each of the institutions just noted brings together guidelines to support the process of the research, and it is necessary for the student to follow them as closely as possible from the start of the research until it is concluded. There will be a requirement to keep to the guidelines beyond the formal end of the research project (Farrell 2005).

For the novice researcher, it can be difficult to know what is right, so the student researcher needs to access and understand his or her university's own ethical research guidelines, which will help him or her gain a clear understanding of the issues involved and how to resolve them.

The student also needs to understand the importance of following the institution's guidelines and the consequences for all involved if the guidelines are not followed. The reputation of the setting and the reputation of the institution in which the student is studying can be damaged if research is not conducted in an appropriate way.

Consent

No one likes to be tricked and research participants are no exception. It is really important that you make it clear just what it is that you are doing, why you are doing it and what is involved. Then you need to give some indication as to how the findings are going to be used. The ethical researcher will always provide information in a clear and transparent format so that participants give their informed consent – that is, they are fully aware of the strategies to be used, their role and potential implications of the research. The student researcher is guided by his or her supervisor and the requirements of his or her institution.

Student researchers may well find that they are conducting research in a setting. In this case, an agreement from the manager or head of the setting is always required; the complexity of early years' settings may require the permission of a range of people – for example, governors, colleagues and parents. This notion of seeking permission from significant gatekeepers is fundamental to ethical research.

When working with children and young people, considerable care needs to be taken with the planning and organization of this consent as they might be considered too young to provide valid agreement. The key issue here is whether they are able to understand the complexities and subtleties of what it means to agree to cooperate in research. Lahman (2008) discusses this in relation to the contested themes of 'vulnerability' and 'competence', considering the relationship between children as research subjects and researchers. The student researcher needs to be very careful here and must avoid confusing a willingness to take part with informed consent. They are not the same thing. Such consent can be provided only by an appropriate adult.

Activity

A student researcher is interested in researching an aspect of reading with a small group of Year 2 children. She intends to extract a group from their regular class. Consider the ethical issues this raises and the procedure which could be followed.

Finally in this section, it is worth reflecting on the identity of children as research subjects; if you are dealing with young humans, then they need to be involved in the processes that you are instigating. This is their right, and it is clearly a breach of their human rights to assume that they are simply there for you. For the student, a priority might be to complete the project, and the children are subjects to enable this to occur. However, the student needs to understand that the research is likely to become increasingly valid if the children are involved. A wise researcher will engage the children with the procedures of the research and construct the plan with the children at the centre of his or her thoughts. It is not acceptable to simply do research *on* children, as the reflective practitioner will be doing research *with* children.

Confidentiality

Privacy must be respected; if you get a market research phone call one evening about 'how you feel over . . . situation x', then you do not expect your name to be there when they publish their findings – for everyone to know what you think.

Equally, in a setting, employees may not feel at liberty to say how they really feel, fearing the reaction of their manager or colleagues. One way of encouraging them is to provide the assurance that their name will not be revealed at any point: this is respecting confidentiality and is essential to the research process.

Confidentiality is about more than not being able to identify participants. It also considers who can access the information gathered. Papers are expected to be kept securely; a locked cabinet is ideal. Any digital information must be stored securely and be password-protected.

This protection goes beyond staff and parents of children in a setting; it also applies to the children who may be involved. It must not be possible to identify the children by name (using a code system helps here – e.g. child A), images (pictures of backs of heads are usually acceptable) and location. You are strongly advised to consult your institution's guidelines as well as the setting's child protection policies.

Activity

What are the ethical issues raised by the behaviour of the nursery staff in the following scenario? Discuss with your colleagues.

Two nursery colleagues were travelling on the bus after a day at work. One child had been particularly challenging, and they were discussing the reasons for this. They were interrupted by the person in front of them who turned round and asked them not to talk about her brother like that.

Right to withdraw

'Just say no' is a common phrase used to help people resist being pressured into doing something that they do not want to do. It applies to research as well, as the student researcher will quickly find out.

Most parents and professionals are busy people who may not have the time to be involved in a research project. It needs to be made clear what they are agreeing to when they give their informed consent and even then – sometimes quite unexpectedly – they may decide that they no longer want to take part. This right to withdraw is part of your contract with the participant. It is their decision to stay or withdraw, and the student researcher needs to remember that participants are volunteers who are giving up their time to help you.

This means that you need to keep their involvement short and relevant. A series of short questions (where you focus on the key ideas and are able to reassure them that it really will take only five minutes of their time) is more likely to be successful than a more lengthy version. For example, sometimes the longer interview will have to end early when something happens to interrupt the conversation; this is frustrating for everyone.

Right to withdraw also applies once the information has been collected. For example, even if a questionnaire has been completed and filed, the participant may still ask for that information to be withdrawn.

Activity

How can you resolve the protection of confidentiality (keeping information anonymous) with the participant's right to withdraw?

To ensure anonymity, some researchers will include a simple coding system (the last four numbers of a mobile phone number is a popular system) so that the participant alone can identify (and possibly withdraw) his or her contribution.

The ethics committee

Following discussions with your supervisor and reaching agreement on an appropriate research topic, you will normally submit a formal proposal to the ethics committee. This will include details of your research methods, materials, anticipated timescale and other relevant information.

In conclusion, this section on ethics has considered some of the key issues you need to address; as with any research, while you act in good faith and make every reasonable effort to get it right, you need to be prepared for things to go wrong. Aubrey *et al.* (2000) suggest that thorough preparation and putting a paper trail of approvals in place ensures that you will be able to explain your reasoning and decision making should that be necessary.

Research methods

Observation skills

This is the starting point for many students in their placement. You may find similar issues being raised by Yates in Chapter Three on how to approach your placement experience. Observations may help you to choose an area of research interest.

Little questions might start with one of these!

Who What Where When How Why

Activity

A student makes several visits to his or her new placement and observes that the children do not seem very interested in their mid-morning snack.
   Suggest themes which could be researched here.

Of course, the student researcher will need to develop the confidence to ask his or her own questions. This example is included to illustrate the idea that a research question may start from a simple, everyday example. The student researcher then finds an interesting question about the children in their setting.

Reflection

You might wish to reflect on the impact of neither colleagues nor children knowing the researcher and how this might affect the quality of their responses.

Questionnaires and interviews

These are popular research methods, used to gather information in quite different ways.

The typical questionnaire will be constructed to be completed quickly, gathering large amounts of information in a short time. Some questionnaires have boxes which can be ticked, while others may ask for a preference to be indicated. They often lend themselves to being summarised through pie charts and similar quantitative displays.

In contrast, interviews may provide the opportunity for the researcher to gather an in-depth understanding of how a participant feels, so they may be considered a more qualitative approach. As Drever (2003) suggests, interviews take time to set up and carry out, so they may be considered more demanding and require great skill and sensitivity.

So there is a balance between these two approaches. Questionnaires are often more superficial but can collect large amounts of information quickly. Interviews may be more informative, but are likely to focus on a smaller range of participants. Student researchers may well find that they carry out both, starting with a broad questionnaire, which is then followed by a face-to-face interview. This follows the pattern of using diverse strategies to provide legitimacy for the research.

Other approaches to research

Case studies

The case study is usually considered to be an in-depth look at an individual, but may be extended to a small group in a collective case study. It may reveal insights into behaviour which other methods cannot see.

However, any findings are likely to be specific to that group and so may not be confidently generalised to a wider setting. Nevertheless, a good case study can support practice and be of great value to practitioners.

Focus groups

This usually involves a conversation between a small group and a researcher. The format is often lightly structured, and you will find that you are listening more than talking. A sensitive researcher needs to be aware of the needs and rights of all group members, ensuring that everyone has a voice. You may need to plan to carry out one-to-one follow-up interviews with individuals at a later date.

Conversations can be recorded using a digital recorder; other times, the researcher will have a note-taker, who can focus on quickly recording responses, allowing the researcher to concentrate on the discussion.

Following the group discussion, you may have a great deal of material to sift through. An analysis of the words said and how they were said may be called a 'discourse analysis', so the researcher may begin to gain an insight into the ways in which the participants think and how they see their world.

Sometimes, clear themes emerge; the challenge for the researcher is to ensure that the material of the discussion remains focused on the topic under investigation. The researcher will have the responsibility of deciding what to include and what to omit; this is the challenge and a huge responsibility. Mac Naughton and Hughes (2009) explore this question in some depth, inviting students to explore what kind of researcher they are.

Narrative approaches

This final section considers a group of strategies, in which the researcher aims to tell a story (narrative) about what is happening in front of him or her. This provides the opportunity for the researcher to be creative, perhaps using photographs, drawings or poetry. Clark *et al.* (2008) illustrate this vividly in the Mosaic approach strategies, where children were listened to in a range of ways – for example, from the photographs they have taken, book-making and map-making. Some may use a diary or journal to record events as they happen, or write up their day afterwards, perhaps in the evening. This is often called a naturalistic observation, as the children are behaving naturally.

Activity

A student researcher is investigating 'the views of practitioners towards outdoor play' in a nursery setting.

Identify a range of research strategies to capture their views and consider the advantages and disadvantages of each. What may be the challenges the researcher encounters?

A variation of the narrative method is where the researcher focuses on one child and follows him or her. We need to make a decision fairly early on in the process whether we are going to stay close with the child; we can then participate in the activities of his or her world. Alternatively, we can observe from a distance, seeing the child behaving independently.

Both these strategies have their strengths and weaknesses, with the researcher needing to decide which is the most appropriate for his or her work. It is always good practice to test your research strategies with a pilot study; this may involve smaller numbers. It will be useful to establish a shorthand that you can use in order to be able to record your observations easily and quickly.

As suggested, the good researcher will use a range of methods (called triangulation) in order to collect his or her material and to increase the rigour of his or her conclusions. This can then be analysed by looking for themes, patterns and trends. If the researcher has been working with a small group of participants, it may be that the conclusions reached apply only to that group in their setting; however, it may be possible to generalise findings to a wider range of similar participants.

Exploring potential research ideas

You will find your supervisor helpful in choosing and clarifying your research topic. Sometimes it is useful for you to have a look at early years' research that has already been undertaken, and these two sites will provide you with a starting point.

Activity

Visit these websites:

1. The European Early Childhood Education Research Association (EECERA) at *www.eecera.org*.
2. The British Educational Research Association (BERA) website at *www.bera.ac.uk*.

List recent topics which are relevant to researching early years' practice in order to drive improvements in provision. You may find that a keyword search will help you.

You may have a particular personal interest in one aspect of your placement or practice. You can use your research interest to become an emerging expert in a particular area of practice, sharing this expertise with anyone who will listen. How you might share your research is discussed at the end of this chapter.

Referring back to an earlier part of this chapter, there was a review of the two main research paradigms. If you are moving into a rather more scientific approach, you may find that when identifying the focus of your project, you could consider presenting it as a *hypothesis*. This is a way of asking your question that attempts to link two aspects of practice – for example, 'Offering free play opportunities in a Year 2 classroom raises happiness indicators in young children.'

You have a hypothesis with two variables – the one you control (the amount of free play time) and the one you measure (happiness indicators).

However, you may find that you are not comfortable with this and would like to explore how children 'feel' about play. In this case, your aim will reflect this and might become something like 'an investigation into children's feelings toward different types of play'.

It should be clear that either approach is appropriate. You will still need to decide which is right for both you and the context in which the research will be carried out.

This section invited you to begin exploring potential research ideas and has attempted to provide you with some focus here.

Planning your research project

Once the research strategy has been approved by the ethics committee and your supervisor, you will need to plan a timeline for each section and keep to this if you can; plan around your calendar and any other potential distractions.

Another significant resource available to you will be your institutional library. Whether you prefer to work with hard copies of books and journals, or prefer them online, make sure that you really do know how to use the resources at your disposal. In addition, most higher education settings will have a specialist librarian who is available to help you when you need something that you cannot find for yourself. See Chapter One to remind yourself of resources, electronic databases and how to access them.

Activity

Visit the library in your institution and find out:

1. The name of the early childhood studies specialist
2. The opening hours of the library.

  Are there any special resources that you can borrow to take into placement – for example, toys and games?

The literature review

You are likely to find that your research question has been asked before in some shape or form so you will need to do some background reading into your topic. Information that is already written on a topic needs to be explored in what is called a literature review. This *existing literature* needs to be examined in order to find out what has already been written about the subject. However, the smart approach is to focus on good material (see Sedgwick in Chapter One). The challenge then becomes how to condense the material into something which can be managed.

A good literature review will explore the issues raised by the research question and attempt to clarify them for the reader. In one sense, you are trying to search for meanings in the literature and should be on the lookout for 'understandings and practices that have been taken for granted' (Mac Naughton 2005:103) and be ready to question them.

As you collect materials it is important to set up a system for keeping track of what you find. Plastic wallets, files on laptops, piles of papers; it does not matter which you prefer as long as you can easily find what you need – there is nothing worse than having a great quote, but no idea where it was from.

You will need to consider the structure of your review. Often people will include definitions of keywords or concepts and some sort of historical review. Then (signposting with headings if you can) move through the debate and into a questioning section, where you can explore the ideas using quotes and ideas from your literature – all appropriately referenced, of course, and in good English. It is usual to write in the third person singular (*It appears that . . .* rather than *I think that . . .*).

In conclusion, you are now in possession of the key issues surrounding your research question and are an emerging expert, confident on what others have found. You will need to consider the specific ethical issues your research generates and complete a document in which you outline how you are going to deal with them.

Operationalizing your research project

You will have achieved permission to undertake your research, you will have gained consent from all relevant parties in the setting and you will be aware of any policy requirements which may impact upon how you conduct your research and yourself.

It is important to recognise that there will be limits to what you can achieve in the time available to you. Most of the research that you read has been completed over lengthy periods of time, often by a team of experienced researchers. You are working on your own with limited resources, and lack of time is your biggest challenge. As such you need to give some significant thought to the population and sampling strategies you plan to use. It is usually good practice to identify the group you are working with in the title of your project. This is known as your *population*. It is all the people who could be involved in your project. However, there may be too many for you to work with in the time you have available, so you need to identify a smaller group: this is a *sample*.

How the sample is chosen needs some thought, as the information you will acquire from them will be applied (or *generalised*) to the population. For this to be reliable, your sample needs to be typical (or *representative*) of your population. To ensure this is the case, you need to consider two things.

1. The *size of the sample:* It needs to be large enough. For example, if you have a population of twenty staff in a setting and you want to interview all of them, you may find that you run out of time. So you could decide on five to interview: 25 per cent of the population will give you a reasonably representative group, and it will not take you too long.
2. The *selection of the sample:* How you select them is important and there are various ways of organizing this. Usually the easiest way is to work with whoever is willing (an *opportunity sample*), or you might set up a system so that you identify a *random sample* (names out of a hat). There are other sampling methods possible, each of which has strengths and weaknesses.

You will need to make these design decisions (and justify them) with support and guidance from your supervisor.

Let us assume that you have considered all the sections so far. You have a good question and have considered the literature surrounding your question. You have designed a way of answering that question and know who you are going to ask to help you.

The final step in this process is to think ahead and consider what you are going to do with the information you collect. There may be answers to questions which you can present in graphs, pie charts or histograms. There may be conversations you have recorded, and you will need to give some thought to how you are going to read between the lines of what people are saying or doing in order to make your interpretation of their behaviour. There may be observations you have made for which you will need to design frequency charts or content charts in order to make it possible to manage the information you have collected.

As part of your analysis, you may be able to reflect on the ways in which people have responded to your investigations and so provided you with a way of pulling it all together. The best discussions usually consider the information which has been collected and draw some simple and direct conclusions from it. Frequent reference to the 'title' question is recommended, so that the discussion remains focused. Do your findings broadly match what others have found or are there differences? What recommendations can you make to settings from what you have found? Are there immediate changes which they could make to improve or are there bigger changes which might be brought to a meeting for discussion? There are no hard-and-fast rules here; you will need to discuss this final section with your supervisor.

Presenting your research project

Each institution will have its own specific requirements in the presentation, so it is critical that you follow the guidance of your supervisor by attending all lectures and seminars available.

The very best research projects will also ensure that they follow the structural guidance for each section, combining this with the assessment criteria that may also be available to you. The main sections will usually follow this sequence.

Title page – completed in full, often including a word count.

Contents page – with page numbers.

Acknowledgements – thanks to those who have helped you.

Outline – an overview and a little personal reflection.

Literature review – the key issues and relevant literature.

Scope and aim – what are you investigating and what do you hope to achieve?

Methodology – how did you carry out your research and respect the ethical guidelines?

Statement of results – what did you find out?

Analysis and discussion – report on the meaning of your results and their implications for practice, together with recognition of the constraints you found. How has the research impacted on both you and your setting?

Summary and conclusions – what are the key outcomes of your work?

References – following the recommended style (e.g. Harvard) and conforming to the writing guidelines of the institution.

Appendices – in which any relevant information is included that has not found a place in the main body of the report.

What can you do with your research?

If you are carrying out your research as a student project, you will have a deadline to meet and it is important to ensure that your work is handed in on time. However, you may want to take your ideas a little further, and there are a number of ways of doing this that you should discuss with your supervisor. The first thing to do on receiving your project following assessment is to read the feedback. This enables you to refine and develop the areas that were felt to be weak. Then you might consider how your findings can be disseminated to a wider professional audience.

You may consider starting with the setting in which the research was carried out, as it is in the setting that your findings will have the most relevance. Your starting point is likely to be the class teacher or manager with whom you work most closely and you should discuss your ideas with him or her. You may then need to present your ideas to other members of staff: be prepared for such meetings and plan for obvious questions that you could be asked. You could consider offering to do a short presentation to a group of staff, perhaps to provide a small number of PowerPoint slides as a summary of your work, to also include any recommendations you consider important. This may sound like rather a daunting challenge, but you have carried out the research and should have confidence in your findings and their meaning; you have the responsibility to share this with colleagues and contribute to the body of knowledge that is early childhood studies. If this is a route you feel able to follow, you might have the opportunity to share your work with colleagues from a range of local settings; there is much to be said for arranging a personal visit to offer a short talk on your findings. This sharing of good practice helps to stimulate debate and at the same time gives you the opportunity to gain valuable experience.

Another direction that you might also consider is to contact an early years' publication and ask them for details of how to have your work featured, either in the printed version or on their website. This way, you will be able to share your research with a readership of many thousands.

So how does that make you feel? In this final section, you have the opportunity to reflect on the impact of carrying out research as a student. It will firstly impact on the way in which co-workers see you in your setting. The ability to identify a question, to then drill down to investigate the issues raised and finally to make recommendations is to identify you as a practitioner with an eye for quality. You are saying that you are not happy to simply accept things as they are, but you have both the *confidence* and *competence* to challenge practice. This identifies you as a particular type of student, one with the potential to develop his or her career in a dynamic and proactive way.

Conclusion

In following the themes of this chapter, it is hoped that you now have a better understanding of what research is and how it can contribute to practice. This chapter has sought to explore the idea that through undertaking research and gathering evidence to support change, it is possible to guide settings in the provision of a higher-quality experience. The voices of very young children may not always be heard in decisions that affect their lives, but through research, we can work towards more effective and frequent ways of listening to them.

References and further reading

Aubrey C., David T., Godfrey, R. & Thompson, L. (2000) *Early Childhood Educational Research: Issues in Methodology and Ethics*. London: Routledge Falmer.

Bell, J. (1998) *Doing Your Research Project*. Maidenhead: OUP.

Clark, A., Kjorholt, A. & Moss, P. (2008) *Beyond Listening*. Bristol: Policy Press.

Coady, M. (2010) "Ethics in Early Childhood Research." In G. Mac Naughton, S. Rolfe, & I. Siraj-Blatchford (eds), *Doing Early Childhood Research: International Perspectives on Theory and Practice* (pp. 73–84). Maidenhead: OUP.

Curtiss, S. (1977) *Genie: A Psycholinguistic Study of a Modern-Day "Wild Child"*. London: Academic Press.

Dahlberg, G. (2007) *Beyond Quality in Early Childhood Education and Care*. London: Routledge.

Denzin, N. & Lincoln, Y. (2005) *The SAGE Handbook of Qualitative Research*. London: SAGE.

Drever, E. (2003) *Using Semi-structured Interviews in Small-Scale Research: A Teacher's Guide*. Glasgow: SCRE.

Farrell, A. (2005) *Ethical Research with Children*. Maidenhead: OUP.

Foley, P. & Leverett, S. (2008) *Connecting with Children: Developing Working Relationships*. Bristol: OUP.

Lahman, M. (2008) "Always Othered: Ethical Research with Children." *Journal of Early Childhood Research* 6 (3): 282.

Mac Naughton, G. (2005) *Doing Foucault in Early Childhood Studies*. London: Routledge.

Mac Naughton, G. & Hughes, P. (2009) *Doing Action Research in Early Childhood Studies: A Step by Step Guide*. Maidenhead: OUP.

Mukherji, P. & Albon, D. (2010) *Research Methods in Early Childhood*. London: SAGE.

Oates, R. & Sanders, A. (2008) "Making a Little Difference for Early Childhood Studies Students." In T. Papatheodorou & J. Moyles (eds), *Learning Together in the Early Years* (p. 187). Abingdon: Routledge.

Rinaldi, C. (2001) "The Pedagogy of Listening: The Listening Perspective from Reggio Emilia." *Innovations in Early Education: The International Reggio Exchange* 8 (4): 4.

Sylva, K. & Taylor, H. (2006) "Effective Settings: Evidence from Research." In G. Pugh & B. Duffy (eds) *Contemporary Issues in the Early Years* (4th ed) (pp. 165–180). London: SAGE.

Van Wynsberghe, R. (2006) "The 'Unfinished Story': Narratively Analyzing Collective Action Frames in Social Movements." *Journal of Qualitative Inquiry* 16: 894–901.

Watson, J. & Rayner, R. (1920) "Conditioned Emotional Reactions." *Journal of Experimental Psychology* 3: 1–14.

Chapter 3

The emerging practitioner

Ellen Yates with Michelle Appleby

By the end of this chapter you will:

- Understand what an emerging practitioner is.
- Have some understanding of recent changes in the early childhood sector and the current context.
- Be able to identify some roles and responsibilities within settings.
- Be able to reflect upon what constitutes professional conduct in preparation for placement.
- Have some knowledge and understanding of safeguarding, health and safety in the setting.
- Understand the role and value of observations and how to manage these in an ethical manner.
- Understand the importance of reflecting on practice.

Introduction

This chapter aims to support students prior to attending work placements who may have little or no experience of working with children. Attending an early years' setting for the first time can be a daunting experience for those with little understanding of early years' practice, and it is important to prepare well and have some idea of what to expect. To the uninitiated and inexperienced, early years' settings can appear at first sight to be noisy, chaotic, confusing places, and it can be difficult to identify exactly how the settings work (roles and responsibilities) and how children gain from the experiences presented (planning and curriculum). It can also be difficult for the volunteer to understand where they fit into the setting and what is expected of them. This chapter intends to support the *emerging practitioner* by demystifying aspects of early years' practice and by answering key questions surrounding early years' practice and the role of the student/volunteer.

It is hoped that by the end of the chapter the reader will develop confidence in his or her ability to successfully negotiate this highly specialised and complex area of practice and be prepared to begin his or her journey as an *emerging practitioner* in an informed and enthusiastic manner.

What is an emerging practitioner?

The title of this chapter, The emerging practitioner, is worth some discussion as it is a relatively new term and may not be understood or produce a 'shared meaning' for all. The first part of the title, *emerging*, is relatively easy to understand as it has a descriptive function and describes similar phenomena when used in different contexts. The *Collins English Dictionary* (2011) defines *emerge* as:

- To come into view
- To become apparent
- To come into existence after a long period of time.

When relating these definitions to practice in early years' settings, then, it is clear that *emerging* relates to *coming into existence* or *becoming independent* in relation to practice. However, the term *practitioner* is more complex as it can be applied in many circumstances and its meaning is dependent upon the context in which it is used. For example, the terms 'nurse practitioner' and 'dental practitioner' describe two distinct professions with very different aspects of practice. A dictionary definition gives little information; a *practitioner* is defined as:

- a person who practises a profession (*Collins English Dictionary* 2011) – *in our case early years practice in working with children.*

A further definition of *practice* illuminates our enquiry further and is defined as:

- repetition of an activity in order to gain skill (ibid.).

Based on these definitions we can construct a shared meaning of the term *emerging practitioner* as being a person *who practices a profession, through repetition in order to achieve skill, resulting in independence.* The emphasis on 'practice' in order to achieve mastery can be understood in many contexts – learning to drive, for example. However, in the field of early childhood, the process is vastly more complex than this as it involves *relationships*, and some have criticised the use of the term 'practitioner' in relation to early years' practice as it '*suggests that work within the early years field is essentially routine and mechanical*' (Browne 2004:3). What is important for the emerging practitioner to understand at this point is that *practice* of working with young children and *theory* related to early childhood are fundamental to becoming competent and confident; one without the other is not sufficient. Another very important idea to understand is that what is important in early childhood differs according to theoretical perspectives and *childhood* is a shifting concept in social and political terms. It follows that *continual review* of practice is fundamental.

The current context

The early childhood sector has enjoyed focused attention over the past decade from the Labour government until May 2010, when power was transferred to a Conservative/ Liberal Democrat coalition. This political focus from the previous

Labour government resulted in huge changes in funding, workforce development (Children's Workforce Development Council & Early Years Professional Status) and curriculum (Early Years Foundation Stage; DfES 2007), as well as the introduction of new legislation and initiatives based on the influential green paper 'Every Child Matters' (DfES 2003b). These changes aimed to improve outcomes for all children through good-quality provision with an emphasis on teamwork and multi-professionals working alongside a commitment to professionalise the workforce in the form of the Early Years Professional Status (EYPS). Farelly (2010) identifies the most significant of these changes as:

- An increase in provision
- The introduction of the Early Years Foundation Stage Curriculum
- The development of a qualification framework
- A graduate-led workforce. (Farelly 2010:17)

(A more detailed and comprehensive overview of the recent history of early childhood can be found in Farelly 2010, chap. 2.)

Prior to these changes, the quality of experience that children received within early years' settings could be very different depending on the type of setting they attended and the staff that were employed in these settings. As Farelly (2010:15) identifies, the quality and availability of provision for children varied.

Prior to full-time education at 4–5 years old, children could stay in home settings with parents, carers or childminders or attend various private or local authority–run settings, including day care, playgroups, nursery schools and preschools. Each of these settings employed a range of different staff. For example, private day care centres employed nursery nurses (qualified to level 3) and unqualified staff with little or no childcare qualifications or experience, whereas nursery schools were mainly managed by teachers (qualified to level 6). Similarly the emphasis in each setting could be very different, with some settings favouring 'care' and 'well-being' and others favouring 'play' (playgroups) or 'education' (private or local education authority–run nursery schools). The knowledge, experience and qualifications of the adults working in these settings was diverse, and differences in training and qualifications were reflected in job titles such as *nursery nurse*, *teacher*, *play leader*, *supervisor*, and *teaching assistant*.

As can be seen from these examples, children could attend a range of different settings before attending school, each with a different emphasis, and may have encountered many different adults in these contexts with specific notions of what was 'best' for children and what their role entailed. The introduction of the Early Years Foundation Stage (DfES 2007) was an attempt to standardise the experiences of all children in early years' settings 0–5 and replaced the previous Birth to Three Matters (DfES 2003a), the Curriculum Guidance for the Foundation Stage (DfEE 2000) and the National Standards for under 8's Daycare and Childminding (DfES 2003b) merging care, education and well-being. This shifted the emphasis in Early Childhood to *holistic learning and development* and meant that all settings were working towards the same goals for all children. It was recognised within the EYFS that aspects of children's lives that had previously been addressed in isolation, such as health, education and well-being, were interdependent and that to provide the best possible outcomes for children, the workforce from different aspects of children's lives needed to work together more closely and improve the sharing of information. When viewed within this context, the term *practitioner* can be understood as an inclusive term which encompasses all adults who work with young children in early years' settings, despite the fact that these adults may have different qualifications and experiences.

What does an emerging practitioner do?

An early years' practitioner is required to perform various tasks and activities in settings with children and adults which demand a vast range of skills, abilities, knowledge and understanding. Despite the introduction of a common framework for holistic learning and development, children and adults are individuals and should be treated as such. It follows that 'practice' will differ in relation to individual needs, settings and contexts and as such there is no common 'practice' that can be employed in every context or for every occasion that will occur. Theories about children's holistic learning and development will help you to develop your own approach to practice, as will experience within the setting. However, one fundamental aspect that is common to all settings is *team working*; working *in relationship* with others is central to practice, and this will be addressed later in the chapter. An emerging practitioner will be required to undertake *practical tasks*, such as cleaning or sorting equipment, for example, as well as *relational tasks* in relationship with children, parents, carers, the core team and other professionals. The practitioner will also be expected to carry out *professional tasks* relating to their role and responsibilities in the setting, such as observation of children and the planning and evaluation of activities. Obviously these aspects will overlap in practice, but it may be helpful to identify these types of tasks in relation to your own experiences.

 Activity: Undertaking tasks in the placement setting

- Think about your work placement and make a list of the *practical tasks, relational tasks* and *professional tasks* that you have observed or undertaken.
- Can you identify tasks that you are not able to perform as a student/ volunteer?
- Can you identify tasks that need to be performed by specific people in the setting?

Reflecting on the foregoing may give an indication of the array of skills, knowledge and understanding that are required and in turn what is involved in developing one's practice. When you have identified some aspects of practice, add them to Table 3.1 and reflect on the questions. You can add to this as your experience

Table 3.1 Practical, relational and professional tasks in early years settings

Type of task	Skills, knowledge and understanding needed?	How will you develop this? Observing others? Reading, research, theory? Trying out own ideas? Practice and repetition?
Practical tasks		
Relational tasks		
Professional tasks		

develops. This table may also help you to identify the roles and responsibilities of specific staff within the setting.

Roles and responsibilities within settings

Pound (cited in Paige-Smith & Craft 2008:41) identifies a range of roles within early childhood settings, including:

- Graduate level managers
- Early years' professionals
- Supervisory staff
- Qualified teachers
- Wider team – including home settings.

Roles and responsibilities are usually identified by the job title and person specifications that are attached to that role. However, the activities involved in working with young children do not always fall into one person's 'role', and responsibilities and tasks are usually shared and interrelated, involving a team of people working closely together. As Pound identifies, '*Early childhood settings are extremely complex and almost everyone involved finds themselves undertaking a wide range of roles*' (cited in Paige-Smith & Craft 2008:44).

Job specifications then often relate to more practical aspects of roles, such as hours of work, holiday entitlement and expected general duties. However, some responsibilities are specific to certain roles and common to all settings – for example, the Special Educational Needs Coordinator (SENCO) and the person responsible for safeguarding children – and it is important for the volunteer to identify these people as soon as possible. All settings employ a '*key person*' system (or something similar) which ensures that each child has a key person with whom they can develop a close, trusting relationship. The key person is usually responsible for tracking his or her allocated children, observing and documenting their progress while in the setting and sharing information with parents, carers and other professionals. This role is complex and '*involves a high level of responsibility for all aspects of the children's development and well being*' (Pound, cited in Paige-Smith & Craft 2008:44).

Although roles and responsibilities overlap and are not always distinct, the Children's Workforce Development Council developed a *Common Core of Skills and Knowledge* (CWDC 2010) for the Children's Workforce. These aspects are expected of all people who work with young children in any context and will be included within your role.

- Effective communication and engagement with children, young people and families.
- Child and young person development.
- Safeguarding and promoting the welfare of the child.
- Supporting transitions.
- Multi-agency working.
- Sharing information. (CWDC 2010)

The role of the student-practitioner

As a student-practitioner you will usually be allocated a mentor, supervisor or 'critical friend' who will provide you with an induction of the setting, and explain what is expected of you. It is important at this point to identify key roles and responsibilities of people in the setting so that you know who to go to for help. You will also need a health and safety briefing, which will be provided by the setting; much of this will be common sense, but it is important to understand and follow all of the setting's policies, procedures and instructions so that you know what to do in an emergency. All settings are accountable to children, parents, carers and the general public and are currently inspected by the Office for Standards in Education (OFSTED), who make visits to the settings and evaluate their practice. The setting will also have policies on aspects of practice, and these are available for parents, visitors and the OFSTED to inspect. It is very important that you read these documents as they provide the underpinning philosophy and values which determine how the setting is run to meet the statutory guidelines. There will also be aspects of practice in the setting that are unwritten, often called the *hidden curriculum or ethos*; these aspects of practice are more difficult to identify and may become apparent only with experience. The hidden curriculum or ethos of the setting describes aspects of practice that develop when members of a team are confident of their role and working towards common goals. It is important to maintain good communication with your mentor at all times; you will need to explain the requirements of your university course with this person, and he or she is your first point of contact if you need help or support. You will soon get used to the routine of your setting and may be allocated specific tasks to complete by your supervisor. If you are unsure of what to do or need to do specific tasks for your coursework, ensure you discuss this with your supervisor first, who can inform you about the setting's planning and integrate your work into existing plans.

How do I prepare for placement?

Before your first day at your placement you may be nervous and unsure of what to expect; being well prepared can help you to feel confident and secure. Complete the following activity.

Before you go to your placement, consider:

- Ten things you will need to find out before you start the placement.
- Ten things you need to find out on your first visit.
- Ten things that will evidence a successful day.

The foregoing activity is designed to make you consider practical aspects that you may take for granted, such as: What time are you expected to arrive? How long will the journey take? What will you wear? (Some settings have specific requirements and dress codes.) It is good practice to find out as much about your setting as possible before you attend. As a volunteer you will be expected to behave as a member of staff; therefore it is worth considering what is involved in *professional conduct* in more detail.

Professional conduct

> *Professionalism often means that a practitioner is able to move thinking and practice beyond what may normally (or naturally) be done by those working outside the profession and/or field of knowledge.*

> Miller *et al.* (2005:25)

Our behaviour in any situation is usually governed by the context. For example, in a library or supermarket it is unlikely that someone would shout very loudly or burst into song, whereas at a music festival this kind of behaviour would be quite acceptable, and expected. In any workplace, there are written and unwritten codes of professional behaviour that the student-practitioner will need to pay attention to. Try the exercise in Table 3.2.

Can you identify any areas for improvement? These could form the basis for a *professional development plan* or PDP, which will be discussed in more detail in later chapters.

Before you attend your placement you will need an Enhanced Criminal Records Bureau (CRB) check, which ensures that you are a *suitable person* to work with young children. This is currently under review, and there are plans to make this process more rigorous in light of recent legislation (Safeguarding Vulnerable Groups 2006). It is important to ensure this is completed in good time before you start your work placement.

Table 3.2 Professional behaviour in early years settings

Try to identify aspects of professional behaviour and add your own examples.

Professional behaviour	Examples
Personal qualities	Patience
	Flexibility
Professional qualities	Confidentiality
	Punctuality
	Professional appearance
Academic qualities	Knowledge about theories of child development

Table 3.3 Effective communication

Eye contact	No eye contact
Clear language	'Jargon' or unfamiliar language
Non-verbal cues – facial expression	

Communication

As Miller *et al.* (2005) identify, effective communication is the basis of good team-work, and this involves the ability to handle conflict in an open and honest manner, as well as the ability to share and celebrate success.

Communication is a key skill in life, and good communication is fundamental to the *emerging practitioner.* As we have discussed, the early years' workforce is made up of a diverse range of professionals, each with individual experiences and expertise; the *emerging practitioner* will need to communicate effectively with these professionals *as well as* with children, parents and carers. This is not an easy task, and you will need to modify how you communicate with each individual; this involves good listening skills as well as good communication skills. You will also need time to discuss your ideas, feelings and developing understanding with your supervisor and colleagues. Communication may include the following aspects:

- *Information* about children and families (some of which will be confidential).
- *Ideas* based on your knowledge and developing understanding.
- *Feelings and opinions*, which need to be clearly distinguished from facts.
- *Observations*, which will be confidential and objective.

It is important to consider *the context, the format and with whom* you need to communicate. Thinking about how you communicate with others may help you identify what contributes to making communication effective. Repeat the following exercise for communicating with different groups in the setting; children, parents and carers, other professionals. List the different people you may communicate with in the table and ways you will communicate with these people. Are there any similarities and differences between groups?

Some examples are provided in Table 3.3 – add your own ideas.

Team working

As Miller *et al.* (2005) identify, good communication is key to good teamwork, as interpretations of events will differ from individual to individual.

> *Working together effectively to meet the needs of children and families means being prepared to listen to different interpretations of what is happening and to modify practice if appropriate. It is vital, therefore, that professionals have regular opportunities to share their knowledge, values and beliefs, and to develop sound understanding and knowledge of what children need to grow and learn.*
> (Miller *et al.* 2005:28)

It is clear, then, that individuals will have their own way of looking at a situation dependent upon knowledge, understanding and experience. This should be seen as a positive opportunity for professionals to view things from another perspective that may not have been considered. Therefore, it is important for all those working with children to share information, ideas and feelings, but these should be communicated in an appropriate manner and within a suitable forum. Some information can be shared in group contexts, such as staff meetings, while sensitive, confidential information may need to be discussed with specific individuals or professionals with specific responsibilities, such as the SEN coordinator or the child's parent/carer. In order for individuals to communicate effectively, however, an open and equitable ethos is vital to ensuring that all members of the team are heard. As Rodd points out, *'better relationships are considered to develop out of feelings of safety, security and trust and are characterised by openness and sharing between people'* (Rodd, cited in Miller *et al.* 2005:29).

In order for the emerging practitioner to develop his or her practice, open dialogue with other professionals is important, as is reflection on practice. This important aspect of practice will be explored in the final section of this chapter and in more depth in later chapters.

Health, safety and risk

The health and safety of children within early years' settings are of paramount importance, yet as Tovey (2007:101) recognizes,

> *the word safe means different things to different people and is dependent on values and perceptions of children and childhood.*

It is clearly part of the setting's responsibility to ensure that children are kept safe and secure, but accidents are a part of life and it could be argued that children need to be exposed to some forms of risk in order to be challenged. Nevertheless, settings need to comply with the statutory requirements outlined in the EYFS and are required to provide suitably qualified staff, an appropriate environment and effective, age-appropriate resources.

Consider your previous experiences and try the following activity.

 What strategies are in place in your setting to ensure children's safety and to minimise risk?
Think about action you have to take as well as embedded policies and procedures. What may be your role in ensuring children are being kept safe?

Some points you might have identified are listed here; add your own examples.

- Security – name badges
- Hazards – wet floors
- Movement in the setting – running in small spaces
- Storage of equipment – sharp objects
- Risk assessments for space and equipment (these must be regularly reviewed by the setting).

If you notice anything that may be a health and safety hazard – for example, a wet floor – alert your supervisor or another member of staff immediately. When planning activities for or with children, you should consider the following:

- Any potential hazards.
- Whether the equipment is safe, age-appropriate and inclusive of all children.
- Whether the environment is safe, age-appropriate and inclusive of all children.

Ask for advice and guidance from your supervisor if you are unsure about any aspect of the activity. Reflect afterwards on how you could have improved the activity. Discussing your ideas with your supervisor will help you to consider aspects that you may not have thought about, and the process will become easier with practice.

Safeguarding children

The Children Act (1989) sets out the legal requirements for practice in relation to the safeguarding of children, and further legislation (Children Act 2004, Childcare Act 2006) has aimed to support those working with children to meet the Every Child Matters outcomes. The EYFS (DfES 2013) sets out statutory guidance for safeguarding and promoting children's welfare. The legal framework requires settings to place the welfare of children at the heart of their practice, and this means identifying and supporting children and families in difficulty. Therefore it is important to be well informed regarding your setting's approach by doing the following:

- Reading your placement's safeguarding children policy and procedure document at the earliest opportunity.
- Identifying the designated person responsible for safeguarding in the setting.

It is important to remember that as a student you should report any concerns you may have about any child to your setting supervisor. The staff in the setting will know the children and their circumstances and will be best placed to make decisions about any information you share with them. It is also paramount to recognise the sensitive nature of any information that you pass on and the ethical issues involved. Information about children and families should be kept confidential and you need to use discretion in sharing this with the appropriate people. If any child discloses sensitive information to you, as a student-practitioner it is imperative that this is reported to your supervisor immediately. Do not be afraid to pass on information to the setting in any circumstance if you think it may be important for the welfare of a child.

When you begin your placement you may well spend much of your time observing others. Initially this will be focused upon staff, routines, activities and the day-to-day organization of the setting. As you become more familiar with the setting and the children in it, you will spend some of your time on focused observations as part of your studies, in order to know them better so that you can support them more effectively and develop your practice. In the following section, Appleby provides some strategies and approaches that you can try for yourself, alongside a discussion of the importance of reflecting upon practice.

Observing children

This section will help you to:

- consider the observer's role with attention drawn to ethical considerations.
- contemplate the importance and difference of and between aims and objectives.
- examine how to record observations.
- consider the appropriate use of different techniques.
- think of the role of reflection as an early years' practitioner.

Practitioners today know that watching children can lead to fascinating conclusions which can best guide practice and individual learning for young children. If the goal is to raise the quality of care that children experience in early years' provision, then observation is the most efficient and reliable way to achieve this. In this section, we will discuss the observer's role and different ways we can watch children, focusing on the appropriate use of different techniques.

The observer's role

Palaiologou (2012) explains that observation is a systematic method of studying human behaviour within a context and that it should always have a clear purpose. There is a wealth of literature available on observing children, and I strongly encourage you to investigate the books which are cited here. Drummond (1998) suggests that we should develop ways of monitoring and recording ways young children interact with each other and with their environment in order to deeply understand who they are as individuals and the learning that is taking place. When observing children it is imperative that the observations be carried out in a logical and systematic way. This takes detailed planning, and conclusions resulting from these observations should be grounded on theory. While observing, the information being recorded should capture as much detail as possible and be factual and accurate. It is very important the observer exercise a non-judgemental and unbiased method of operating and address ethical issues, including seeking permission from the setting and ensuring the child's identity remains confidential (Riddall-Leech 2005).

Ethical implication of observations

Before starting to observe in any setting, careful thought should be given to children's right to participate or not (Palaiologou 2012) as well as other ethical considerations. In order to consider the ethical implications of observing children, we need to be sure we understand the purpose for these observations. Ethical consent needs to consider who participates in the research, what the research will be used for and how long and where the data will be kept. These practices will vary from setting to setting, so it is imperative for you as an emerging practitioner to identify what these practices are and how you operate within them.

It may be difficult to avoid identifying the setting or child while making observations. Because of ethical considerations, many practitioners address this issue by referring to the child by their first initial and by referring to the setting by using a generic title such as The Nursery. It is important as well to remember that any images used remain anonymous throughout the observation and subsequent report. Under the requirements of the Data Protection Act, practitioners must keep all information securely stored. Think of what happens to your observations and reflective diary outside of placement. Are your participants protected in terms of their identity and personal information?

> Locate the ethical guidelines written for your setting and university. What do they say about confidentiality, photography and data storage? Is there any other information that has implications for you as a student-practitioner?

While working in placements and observing children it is always paramount that you follow the setting's policies and procedures. It is advised that you seek permission from the head teacher or supervisor as well as the primary caregiver to the children before you begin any observations. It may even be necessary to inform parents that the observations will be taking place so they can opt out of the process should they choose to do so. The best person to help you navigate these ethical boundaries is your placement supervisor.

Before beginning your observations and after seeking permission, it is necessary to decide if you have all the necessary equipment and resources that you will need. Also, it is worth considering if you have enough time to carry out your research and if you have identified aims for the observation. You will need to have researched a specific observation technique and feel confident that you can carry out the technique and record information simultaneously.

Other things to consider when planning your observations are the time of day, the ratio of adults to children and the location of the observer. Some children have an optimal engagement time early in the day, and others will feel best towards the end of the day. All activities should be well structured and supported before young people are asked to complete tasks independently (Vygotsky 1978). Adults should be nearby to help ensure successful opportunities for the children. If there are not enough adults in the room to ensure success, then observations may not be a true reflection of abilities. Where you are located in relationship to the child being observed will have an impact on your interpretation of the data. Observations are most effective when the observer is located in a discreet location so the child does not feel as if he or she is 'performing' for the observer, thus ensuring more authentic responses on the part of the child. However, ensuring you are located close enough to hear all relevant information is imperative as well. It is a difficult balance to remain discreet and still close enough to effectively record what is being observed.

Many times in a busy early years' setting spontaneous observations are the most valuable as they capture moments which may otherwise be missed. Remember to remain as objective as possible in these situations and take time to reflect on and interpret the data you captured as soon as possible after the observation. Draw upon relevant theories, academic sources and milestones of development and curriculum frameworks to help you in interpreting the data. All student-practitioners are encouraged to discuss their findings with other professionals and practitioners to help them interpret their results.

Aims and objectives

Aims and objectives help you to focus your observation, making it possible for you to evaluate and compare your results to previous research or the wider body of knowledge already in existence. Sometimes for emerging practitioners it is difficult to understand the difference between an aim and an objective. Aims refer to the general area you are observing, such as physical ability or fine motor control. Aims tend to be more general, addressing the question, 'What are you looking for?' Be sure to keep the aims focused on the child and concise in the wording.

Objectives tend to be more specific, focusing particularly on the area you want to observe, such as how an eight-month-old baby uses his or her hands to play with a soft ball. An objective tends to be a very particular skill you are looking for in the observation. This skill or goal is usually measurable and detailed, thus denoting a reason for the observation in the first place.

> Before carrying out an observation it is important to develop and formulate its aims and objectives. This ensures that the observed information will be focused and can be effectively used to assess the child's development and to plan appropriate activities and experiences.
>
> (Riddall-Leech 2005:15)

Essential information to be included in your observation is the date and the start and finish time of the observation. Also include the name of the child that you will be using throughout the observation (for ethical reasons, consider using an initial), include the exact age of the child in years and months and denote the observation method used, the aim and objectives of the observation and the number of adults and children in room. The context of setting is also important to consider. Many practitioners use an already made observation form to note this information. At the end of the observation, you will form a conclusion reflecting your aim and objectives as well as an evaluation referring to developmental milestones with recommendations for future practice.

Observational strategies

Observation requires a plan of action and a predetermined format for recording information. There are many different types of observations, but no one technique will fulfil all of the requirements needed to plan and evaluate interactive and engaging programmes for children. It is important to be able to recognise the opportunities and challenges of each type of observational strategy, and the best way to do this is by trying them out. Often working on different observation techniques is a valuable way to spend placement hours and could offer useful information for the programme leader if shared. A beneficial way to build up a multifaceted view of a child is to use several strategies over time. Narratives, checklists, sampling, diagrams and charts are all different ways of carrying out observations. Each one will be discussed in turn.

Narratives are a way to capture information which is rich and has depth. They tend to read like a running commentary of what the child did, often written in the present tense. Positioning of the researcher is imperative when carrying out this technique as the researcher should not become involved in the activities with which the child is involved (Riddall-Leech 2005). There are several different types of narrative as they can be structured and unstructured, in a diary or case study format. The benefits include the ability to record behaviours and activities spontaneously; being able to focus in depth on one particular person can generate rich data, but if the child becomes aware he or she is being observed it can skew the accuracy of the data.

Checklists can include pre-coded charts based often on indicators dictated by theories. They require pre-observation planning as the objectives are presented in list form prior to the observation based on developmental milestones. These are frequently used in early years' settings and are often a good way to engage parents in the assessment process. Some local authorities may produce these for children in a setting to be used to assess whether children are reaching milestones in a timely manner. They are quick and easy to use to compare the attainment of one child compared to averages of children locally or nationally. However, they record only what the child did and not how the child went about doing the activity and are, therefore, of limited use.

Sampling can entail time sampling, whereby an observation is made at predetermined time intervals, or event sampling, whereby an observation occurs anytime certain behaviour is observed. These strategies can be structured and unstructured, in a diary or case study form, and can be used for a wide range of different purposes, such as social interactions and language development. It is clear and easy to use, but the observer needs to have a degree of familiarity with codes. Because of the preplanning involved these types of operations would be challenging to do spontaneously.

Diagrammatic strategies may include bar charts, pie graphs, socio-grams and flow charts. They represent the data in visual form and can present results for larger groups of children. They are useful for tracking children's choice of activities in an early years' setting and are usually easy to read. Construction of these items may require enhanced ICT (Information and Communication Technology) skills, and they may require some sort of written commentary to supplement it.

Socio-grams are a type of chart used for recording children's social interactions. Some practitioners think that these types of recording devices are not true observations, as they do not record any behaviours or activities (Riddall-Leech 2005). The information gathered is recorded on a pre-made chart. It is important as a practitioner to think critically about what gets recorded here, and perhaps recording this information on more than one occasion is more useful. Children can be easily influenced in their friendship choices, often choosing friends who have had a recent birthday or have acquired a new toy. Socio-grams are straightforward to use and useful for finding patterns in classes of children, but they require pre-planning and capture information only in one moment.

Activity

Read the following case study.

Sara is three years old and has just moved to the area and joined her nursery class within the last month. Her caregivers have noticed that she is reluctant to verbally communicate with anyone at the setting. She does seem to love to play on her own and has communicated non-verbally with the practitioners and other children. Her peers are keen for her to join in during playtimes, but she is often on the periphery of the activity watching the others. Her caregivers have enquired about Sara's language development at home, and they have been reassured she is quite verbal with her parents. The practitioners are quite concerned as to why she has not spoken in the nursery setting and have decided to undertake some observations to help them answer this question.

Decide which observation techniques you would use to observe the child. What is your rationale for using that technique? What are the advantages and disadvantages of this method? Could you have used a different technique?

It is important to remember that we must try to remain as objective as possible when interpreting the implication of an observation. Consider the following quotation:

> In order to make the most honest observations and evaluations that we can, we need to take our own beliefs into account . . . this examination of self requires effort and will on the part of the observer.
>
> (Willan *et al.* 2004:111)

As you think about the implication of this quotation, consider a child playing alone on a playground. Do you see 'a loner', a 'self-sufficient child' or a 'confident individualist'? Will this view you hold of children playing alone influence any conclusions you will come to regarding this child? It is important as well to remember that the ultimate goal of observation is to raise the standard of practice for provision of young children, and all conclusions and recommendations which are derived from observations of children should suit this purpose.

It is right to be mindful that an observation is like a camera shot, and although what you observe and the conclusion you draw from those observations are real and true, they may not be fully representational of the child all the time (Nutbrown 2011). It is important to refrain from making judgements about children based on your observations, especially if they are a 'one-off'.

The reflective process

As an emerging practitioner, one of the main areas of focus as you begin to work in the early years' sector will be the process of reflection. For many practitioners this will be the first time they will have done this. As you begin to develop this skill, it is recommended that you are meticulous about identifying areas of your practice on which you reflect and actually write your reflections down. Many practitioners find this tedious and time-consuming as there are many more pressing matters which need attention in an early years' setting. However, it is advised that you reconsider your position, as personal and professional reflection is an element of every truly outstanding practitioner's craft (Smidt 2005).

Many may not even know what a reflection is and how to demonstrate reflection in writing. It is the aim of this section to give you more information about reflection and how to develop this skill as an emerging practitioner in the early years' sector.

True reflection involves the process of observing oneself and the behaviours, thoughts and feelings that are involved in an interaction or event and using those observations to inform future practice. It is about thinking about your thinking, also called metacognition. Reflective learning is one of the most valuable learning experiences we can undertake as it requires us to learn from our own experiences and actions (Reed & Canning 2010).

It is easier to start reflecting on one lesson or interaction when you first start off. Try this:

Think about one interaction or lesson you have had with a young child. Think about what went well during the interaction. Now, think about what you might have done differently. Was there any moment which had the potential to change your thinking about the future?

Biggs and Tang (1999) say that reflection is the most challenging of all cognitive skills. It ranks high on the list, alongside analysing information and application of information to new situations. Interestingly, it is a skill which practitioners often are expected to know how to do with little to no instruction or preparation.

Many practitioners are reflecting without even knowing it. One may kneel down to talk to a child and the child may respond well to this. The practitioner subconsciously is aware that the interaction was successful and valuable for the child but may not have identified the reasons why. The practitioner may also use this first experience communicating with children to influence further interactions communicating with young children. However, the practitioner has not taken the time to think about why this interaction was so successful and will influence future practice (Basford & Hodson 2011). This practitioner has followed his or her instinct, which is excellent. The next step to improving practice is taking the time to record the reflection to inform future interactions, thus increasing the quality of the experiences for children. The importance of recording reflections, even in a busy setting, cannot be overstated.

Experienced practitioners are aware of the many ways in which they reflect and use these skills daily to improve the quality of care and education for children in their setting. Reflection is a process which, like most things, becomes easier the more you do it. The ultimate goal of reflection is to improve your practice. There are many types of reflection. Reflection can occur as a moment is unfolding or after an event (Schon 1983). It can have a 'sense of exploration' as you try to find out more about an idea or it can involve critically thinking about a topic which is 'active and deliberate' (Moon 2008:26). Bolton (2005) says that reflective thinking can involve how your actions are perceived by others. There are many interpretations of the word reflection.

Think for a moment about what reflection means to you as it relates to events which you have experienced and then decide if any changes could be made to improve your practice.

Remember reflection is not just about coming to substantial conclusions. It could be that you make a small change which may have a significant impact on the children in your care.

Reflection encourages us to examine our areas for development, our strengths and our potential resources. It requires an ability to accept that there is still more to learn and more knowledge to acquire. Reflection forces us to examine our weakness and identify areas for improvement.

It involves examining what you do as a practitioner, how you respond to adults and children, how you plan, how you carry out the plan, how you revise the plan for next time, what went well, what did not go well and why did it not go well and using all this information to plan for the future.

 Using a reflective diary

We encourage all student-practitioners to use a reflective diary to support their studies; this can be a notebook of any kind. You may find a handbag-sized notebook more useful. You will need to observe all the foregoing ethical guidance when making notes and comments.

You may find that several of your assessments require you to evidence reflection in practice, and keeping a diary will help you develop your ability to critically reflect on your emerging practice.

For further advice and guidance see Paige-Smith and Craft (2008).

Chapter summary

In this chapter we have considered what it means to be an *emerging practitioner* and identified ways to support you in this role. We have explored roles and responsibilities within settings and aspects of professional conduct, including communication, health and safety, risk and safeguarding. The importance of teamwork has been highlighted alongside the need for careful observation of children and reflection on practice. You have been encouraged to maintain a reflective diary in support of your studies, taking account of ethical guidelines and best practice. It has been our intention to both inform and empower the *emerging practitioner* on his or her journey towards becoming a *developing practitioner* and eventually *a critically reflective practitioner*, each of which will be explored in the following chapters.

References and further reading

Basford, J. & Hodson, E. (2011) *Successful Placements in Early Years Settings*. Exeter: Learning Matters.

Biggs, J. & Tang, C. (1999) *Teaching for Quality Learning at University*. London: Open University Press.

Bolton, G. (2005) *Reflective Practice: Writing and Professional Development*. London: SAGE.

Browne, N. (2004) *Gender Equity in the Early Years*. Maidenhead: Open University Press.

Childcare Act (2006) Available from www.legislation.gov.uk/ukpga/2006/21/contents. Date accessed 6-7-13.

Children Act (2004) Available from www.legislation.gov.uk/ukpga/2004/31/contents. Date accessed 6-7-13.

Children's Workforce Development Council (2010) *The Common Core of Skills and Knowledge*. Available from http://dera.ioe.ac.uk/512/1/CWDC. Date accessed 6-7-13.

Collins English Dictionary (2011) Available from www.collinslanguage.com/results.aspx? context = 3&reversed = False&action = define&homonym = 0&text = emerge. Date accessed 6-22-11.

DfEE/QCA (2000) *Curriculum Guidance for the Foundation Stage*. London: QCA.

DfES (2003a) *Every Child Matters*. London: TSO.

DfES (2003b) *National Standards for under 8's Daycare and Childminding*. Nottingham: DfES Publications.

DfES (2007) *The Early Years Foundation Stage: Setting the Standards for Learning, Development and Care for Children from Birth to Five*. Nottingham: DfES Publications.

DfES (2013) *Statutory Framework for the Early Years Foundation Stage*. Available from www. foundationyears.org.uk/early-years-foundation-stage-2012. Date accessed 6-7-13.

Drummond, M.J. (1998) Observing Children, in Smidt, S. (ed.) *The Early Years: A Reader*. London: Routledge.

Farelly, P. (2010) *Early Years Work Based Learning: A Guide for Students of Early Years and Early Childhood Studies*. Exeter: Learning Matters.

Miller, L., Cable, C. & Devereux, J. (2005) *Developing Early Years Practice*. London: David Fulton.

Moon, J. (2008) *Critical Thinking: An Exploration of Theory and Practice*. London: Routledge.

Nutbrown, C. (2011) *Key Concepts in Early Childhood Education and Care*. London: Sage.

Paige-Smith, A. & Craft, A. (2008) *Developing Reflective Practice in the Early Years*. Maidenhead: Open University Press.

Palaiologou, I. (2012) *Ethical Practice in Early Childhood*. London: Sage.

Reed, M. & Canning, N. (eds.) (2010) *Reflective Practice in the Early Years*. London: SAGE.

Riddall-Leech, S. (2005) *How to Observe Children*. Oxford: Heinemann.

Safeguarding Vulnerable Groups (2006) Available from www.legislation.gov.uk/ukpga/2006/4/ contents. Date accessed 6-7-13.

Schon, D. (1983) *The Reflective Practitioner: How Professionals Think in Action*. New York: Basic Books.

Sharman, C., Cross, W. & Vennis, D. (2004) *A Practical Guide to Observing Children*. 3rd ed. London: Continuum.

Smidt, S. (2005) *Observing, Assessing and Planning for Children in the Early Years*. London: Routledge.

Tovey, H. (2007) *Playing Outdoors, Spaces and Places, Risk and Challenge*. Maidenhead: Open University Press.

Vygotsky, L.S. (1978) *Mind in Society*. Cambridge, MA: Harvard University Press.

Willan, J., Parker-Rees, R. & Savage, J. (2004) *Early Childhood Studies*. Exeter: Learning Matters.

Chapter 4

The developing practitioner

Christine Hey

By the end of this chapter you will:

- Understand the difference between an emerging and a developing practitioner.
- Have an understanding of some theories of reflection.
- Know how to approach a new placement and how to negotiate your departure from a placement.
- Know how to manage academic work in placement.
- Know how to use a Professional Development Plan (PDP) to help support your development in placement.
- Understand the importance of professional relationships in placement.
- Know what to do if a placement is not working for you.
- Be able to access further reading.

Introduction: how does a developing practitioner differ from an emerging practitioner?

In Chapter Three, Yates and Appleby support the emerging practitioner by introducing key skills of observation, managing observations in placement and introducing theories of observation. Thus, student-practitioners emerge with greater knowledge of what children do, how they learn and how they play. Their observations help them to see how the setting meets the children's needs.

Emerging practitioners can, then, confidently observe and record their findings. They know that quality observations underpin and drive forward effective provision.

So, the student-practitioner begins to make sense of the busy, multilayered experience that is an early years' setting and is more confident of his or her place in it. As Willan (cited in Parker-Rees *et al.* 2010:63) states,

> For early childhood students, learning to become competent observers is crucial. Close observation of children helps to link theory and practice and provides a base from which to challenge current theories . . . to be a good observer involves learning to stand back, to suspend judgement, to watch, and, above all, to listen.

However, as Willan (cited in Parker-Rees *et al.* 2010), Selbie and Wickett (cited in Parker-Rees *et al.* 2010), Appleby (cited in Reed & Canning 2010) and Paige-Smith and Craft (2008) all note, if observations are to be valid, they must inform deeper thinking (reflection) about what the child does, what the child knows and what the child needs.

So, the developing practitioner needs now to develop reflective practice – that is, to ask the 'W' questions: Who, What, Why.

- Who did what?
- Why did they do it?
- What happened?
- Why did it happen?
- What could be done differently?
- What was my role in this situation?
- Was it the most appropriate role?
- What was I reacting or responding to?

As you can see, once you start asking questions, more questions emerge. This can be likened to Russian nesting dolls; you see what is on the outside, but the story continues in multi-layers on the inside. In essence this is about developing confidence in seeing the context of actions and activities. Selbie and Wickett (cited in Parker-Rees *et al.* 2010:86) suggest the following:

> Developing a genuinely enabling environment in the early years is not an easy task; it requires recognition not just by practitioners, but also by external agencies and policy-makers of the multi-faceted nature of the term 'environment' as well as an appreciation of the complexity of the different forms that environments can take.

In short, the student-practitioner needs to be aware that environments and the activities and conversations within them do not exist in isolation; rather, they may be the result of different views and expectations, policies and principles. This is discussed further in Chapter Five, The enabling practitioner.

Example:

An early years' setting provides creative activities in a conservatory attached to the main single-storey building. It is quite small, so each group visits at specific timetabled opportunities. Because it is a separate room, the children can access it only when there are enough staff to cover both the conservatory and the Base Room.

This morning, two practitioners have rung in sick. Rather than lose their creative opportunity, Ducklings and Goslings decide to combine their teams and take all the children into the conservatory.

The student-practitioner notes in her reflective diary that the room was overcrowded, and the children were cross and impatient because they had to wait for the easel and the activity table.

On reflection, during a tutorial, she was encouraged to ask the following questions:

- Was the result (the children's experience) worth the effort?
- Why did the staff consider the creative experience so important?
- What else could they have done?

From these questions, the student-practitioner was encouraged to reflect upon the notion of creativity being a separate experience, requiring a different room. Where did this idea come from?

It also requires courage because if the status quo is not working, can the reflective practitioner choose to ignore it or must he or she seek new ways forward?

So, as the foregoing example demonstrates, the student-practitioner discovered that the surface problem – that of limited access, vulnerable to cancellation – may arise from an agreed or presumed consensus about what creativity is and where creativity should happen. Or, she may discover that the separation of creativity arises from practical issues such as environmental constraints in the Base Rooms – space, flooring or a reluctance to have 'mess' in the Base Rooms.

Thus, each Russian nesting doll is lifted out and more possibilities emerge which may need discussion or resolution, but the key factor is that the developing practitioner took time to record the initial experience and then reflect upon it.

Reflective practice: what is it?

At its simplest, reflective practice is an activity in which most professionals engage, even if they are unaware that they do so. It may be at the most basic level; a practitioner sits down in the staff room and sighs 'What a morning! They (the children) are so excitable. They're not settling to anything.'

COLLEAGUE 'Yes, it's been the same in Tadpoles. It's always the same in windy weather.'
PRACTITIONER: 'Yes, I wonder why that is? Funny, isn't it? They always want to run around and shout when it's windy.'
COLLEAGUE: 'Shall we go out earlier, then? Give them more time outside?'
PRACTITIONER: 'That's a good idea.'

In a simple conversation, both practitioners have noted a common experience, identified a possible cause and agreed on a response which they believe will meet the children's needs. Leeson (cited in Parker-Rees *et al.* 2010:180) describes it as 'taking the opportunity to think about the work we are doing, either as we do it or after we have done it' and also suggests that in undertaking reflection we can learn from it how our actions and decisions impact upon ourselves and others.

Pause for thought

When did I last reflect either by myself, or with a colleague, upon what I have done or seen in placement?

Appleby (cited in Reed & Canning 2010:11) suggests that being a reflective practitioner involves several components, which she lists as:

- reflection – a term used broadly to describe feelings and thoughts about experiences and actions, with the intention of developing new insights.
- reflective learning – keeping an open mind, wanting to find out more.
- reflective thinking – thinking to or with a purpose, deliberate or subconscious thought.
- reflective writing – an expression and stimulus for 'further reflective thinking'.
- reflection action; 'which informs and is informed by other processes'. Appleby (cited in Reed & Canning 2007:11)
- meta-reflection – 'making the process of reflection explicit' – that is, reflecting upon the act of reflection. Appleby (cited in Reed & Canning 2007:11)

Leeson (cited in Parker-Rees *et al.* 2010:171) defines reflective practice as 'the importance of thinking over one's actions, past and present and identifying the lessons learnt for future action' and further maintains that reflective practice 'should be a crucial aspect of professional work and life-long learning'.

Schon (cited in Willan *et al.* 2010) distinguishes between:

- Reflection *in* action
- Reflection *on* action.

The first takes place while we are *doing* something and the second occurs *after* we have done it. Schon suggested that reflective practice is used by practitioners when they meet (encounter) something or some situation that is new (unique), when previous learning or experience may not be able to help them.

Furthermore, Leeson (in Willan *et al.* 2007) agrees with Schon's distinction and makes the further point, already noted in Chapter Two, that failure to participate in reflection may lead to ill-informed and potentially dangerous practice. So, if practitioners feel unable or unrequired to reflect upon new and challenging experiences, they may fail to build up a bank of knowledge and awareness; thus, every situation has the potential to cause disarray or anxiety rather than providing opportunities to draw upon prior experience. Within these insecure circumstances, children's experiences may be made vulnerable to poor practice and poor decision making.

There may be a culture of avoiding new challenges for fear of creating new workloads or new expectations, where theory and knowledge are seen as threatening and subservient to experience. However, given the right culture of positive critical, creative reflection, such knowledge may be liberating.

Schon, however, offers a further caution, talking about what he called 'technical rationality, where knowledge is divorced from experience' (cited in Willan *et al.* 2007:180). This relates to settings where the values underpinning professional practice are never questioned. This may be disguised as 'common sense', in which beliefs and judgements remain unchallenged by theory or knowledge and habitual practice continues without due regard for new knowledge, new awareness or even new legislative requirements.

This 'head in the sand' approach compromises best practice because it may be based upon historical practice – that is, 'we've always done it this way', which ignores new knowledge or emerging practice.

Reflect

Have you seen or participated in practice that is contrary to what you are learning in your studies? These may be activities or patterns of provision that appear to ignore new knowledge about how children learn, socialise and develop.

Think about ethics when reflecting on placement.

Models of reflective practice

Models of reflective practice help practitioners to scaffold or structure their thinking; they provide opportunities to reflect, document and revisit practice, thoughts and responses.

Kolb (cited in Willan *et al.* 2007) offers one of several cyclical models (Lewin 1946 and Gibbs 1988 cited in Willan Parker-Rees *et al.* 2007); this model is worked through systematically, with equal importance given to each stage. Kolb developed the term 'experiential learning' to describe this process. See Figure 4.1.

Pickles (cited in Willan *et al.* 2007) notes, however, that there was some criticism that the cyclical process undervalued the critical role of reflection itself, by giving it no more than equal status with the other two components. He writes that greater emphasis should be given to Stage 2 – that is, the reflection on experience. However, the cyclical model (Figure 4.2) does reflect the observation guidance that emerging practitioners become familiar with, as Sharman *et al.* (2004) note: observations must be robust, evaluated and used to improve provision for the child.

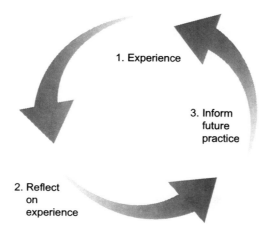

1. Experience

3. Inform future practice

2. Reflect on experience

Figure 4.1 Reflective cycle

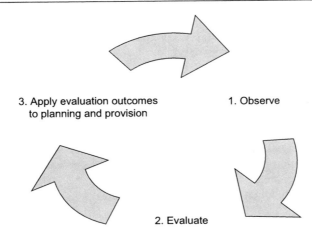

3. Apply evaluation outcomes
to planning and provision

1. Observe

2. Evaluate

Figure 4.2 Cycle of observation and evaluation to inform planning

So it may be argued that a reflective model which resonates with practice could be useful to developing practitioners. However, it may also be argued that the cyclical model does exactly that – the practitioner goes round and round; student-practitioners may need encouragement to step outside of their experiences and take a wider view of their practice. Where observations and reflection *are* closely linked, both must serve a purpose; if observation makes no difference, it is hardly worth the time achieving it. As an emerging practitioner, you may have struggled to plan for the next stage once you have observed and collected data, but as Devereux (in Miller *et al.* 2010:72) states, 'Some kind of action should normally be a consequence of those observations; even if it is a decision to do nothing yet, or to gather further observations before planning changes in provision.'

So, developing practitioners may begin to reflect upon their practice but find themselves within a cycle – a circle – and need some support to take a wider view which enables them to reflect in a way that makes the decision for change, further reflection or knowledge easier to identify.

Seidel (1996 *in* Dempsey *et al.* 2001 cited by Leeson, in Parker-Rees *et al.* 2010) offers an alternative model, which she suggests promotes deeper introspection and thought. She maintains that it has been used to great effect, improving practitioner confidence and skills; see Figure 4.3.

Seidel's model (1996)

The experience is placed in the centre of the model and the four areas of scrutiny are applied – practitioners may not reflect on all four at any one time, but recognise that doing so will widen their thinking and potentially open up new considerations.

- In looking inwards, they reflect upon themselves, their own judgements, values and actions.
- In looking backwards, they reflect upon the context of the experience – its history if you like. Where did it come from? What other influences were at work?

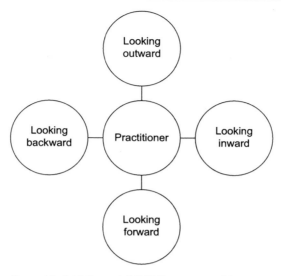

Figure 4.3 Seidel's model (1996), interpreted by Hey

- In looking outwards, they may reflect upon the circumstances around the experience and the response of others to the experience.
- In looking forwards, they reflect upon what they have learnt and consider how can this be shared for best practice. How can a similar situation be avoided or promoted?

Of particular value in this model of reflection is the recognition that we do not work or practice in isolation; we are part of wider teams, working within specific contexts, in particular times. What this model can offer, then, is responsible reflection while avoiding self-destructive criticism. This is important because, as Leeson in Willan *et al.* (2007:186) cautions,

> Reflective Practice is, potentially, a risky business and many are reluctant to engage – we are taking the time to challenge ourselves, demand answers for ourselves and look critically at parts of ourselves that we take for granted.

Seidel's model, then, invites the practitioner to scan through 360 degrees to see the experience from all angles.

Question

How often do you invite the children to reflect upon practice? How can we encourage children to participate in supported reflective practice?

The spiral model (Ghaye & Ghaye, cited in Willan et al. 2007)

Emerging practitioners may be familiar in a different context with the Learning Spiral, advocated by Vygotsky and developed by Bruner into the theory of 'scaffolding'. What these theorists suggested is that in learning and assimilating knowledge,

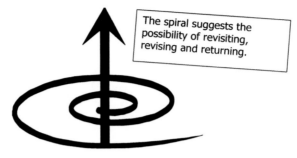

The arrow indicates
That through effective
Reflection, the practitioner
continues to develop.

The spiral suggests the
possibility of revisiting,
revising and returning.

Figure 4.4 The spiral model

children need to revisit and revise their knowledge and understanding, and, with appropriate and sensitive support, they can move from their current knowledge level to the next step (Page *et al.* 2013).

The spiral model (see Figure 4.4), may be hugely useful to the developing practitioner because it not only allows this same level of freedom to revise and revisit but also suggests that a mentor or critical friend can help the reflective practitioner to new levels of understanding.

This is a spiral of action or thought, which allows practitioners to revisit different steps and develop ideas as they progress from one part of the cycle to another.

Its advantage is that practitioners can step back into the reflective cycle at any time and reflect again about the experience; they may have new information, which informs their understanding of the experience. They may realize that their initial response did not take into account all the information available. Just as Piaget's theory of accommodation and assimilation (Page *et al.* 2013) suggested that children need to revisit their learning to adapt it, secure it and effectively build upon it so the spiral model of reflection allows the practitioner to revisit any part of the experience and secure his or her understanding of it, leading to adaptation and learning.

Leeson (cited in Parker-Rees *et al.* 2010:184) further notes that practitioners may need a structure or framework to support their developing reflective practice and offers the following stages.

Stages of reflection

- *Descriptive* – giving an account under scrutiny.
- *Perceptive* – making links between description and feelings.
- *Receptive* – allowing oneself to be open to different perspectives on the incident described.
- *Interactive* – creating links between learning and future actions.
- *Critical* – questioning accepted practice in a creative and constructive manner.

You can see how, using this framework, your reflective writing can move from being merely descriptive to demanding more of you and resulting in more secure evidence for challenge, change or modification.

Activity

Look at a sample from a previous reflective diary or observation and highlight which of the foregoing components are present.

Now try utilising what you have learnt so far to develop your critically reflective writing – that is, reflection, which looks at the situation or experience in greater depth and from a wider perspective (see Figures 4.1, 4.2, 4.3 and 4.4).

How can reflective practice be achieved?

As the foregoing activity will have demonstrated, a key requirement for effective reflective practice is time. Space is also required – not just physical space but also mental and emotional space (Paige-Smith & Craft 2008).

Practitioners need to respect their colleagues' need for reflection and their desire to share and have a common commitment to integrity. Open mentoring – that is, having a critical friend, who will listen and ask non-judgemental questions within a safe and respectful space – is highly supportive. However, Leeson (in Willan *et al.* 2007:179) further notes that reflection carries its own risks – it may be misunderstood and it may seem self-indulgent, rather than 'an opportunity to put academic theory into a real context'.

Reflection may also provoke uncomfortable feelings, challenge a practitioner to change practice or, at the least, challenge current practice (Leeson cited in Willan *et al.* 2007; Moss cited in Paige-Smith & Craft 2008).

Many early years' practitioners have a hugely vocational commitment to their employment, investing a great deal of themselves – their humour, respect, affection, professionalism, time and energy – in the job. Reflecting upon their values, ethos and practice may give rise to strong personal feelings of inadequacy, resentment or anxiety.

The student-practitioner is in a privileged position; they are expected to observe, question and critique what they see and do. They have a tutor to provide professional mentoring and have the time and space to develop their reflective skills.

Summary

You have been introduced to some models of reflection.

You have undertaken some activities to help you explore these models.

You have seen the links between observation and reflection.

You have seen how being a student-practitioner – a developing practitioner – enables you to access time, space and mentoring to support you in your journey.

Furthermore, student-practitioners are expected to apply theory to practice, and this skill is seen as both necessary and of immense value.

Why reflection?

Now that you have been introduced to some key components of reflective practice – its structures, frameworks and potential – we need to consider in greater depth why reflective practice is so important and what it means for you as a developing practitioner.

Activity:

What is a professional?
Write down in one sentence your definition of a professional.

Why is it important for you to reflect upon professionalism and being a professional? In the last few years, there has been a significant commitment to developing a professional early years' workforce. The rise of early childhood studies as an academic discipline, the Labour government's commitment to a world-class children's workforce (DfES 2005) and the introduction of work-based learning in Foundation Degree provision and Early Years Professional Status have all contributed to this notion of professionalism (Farrell 2010). In 2012, Nutbrown undertook an extensive review of the qualifications for early years' practitioners and also looked at professionalism and maintaining and sustaining a high-quality work force. She noted the crucial importance of this shared professionalism and confidence, stating, 'We need to move towards a greater sense of professional roles and identities, ensuring that early years staff have clear and intelligible roles, responsibilities and status, which are understood across the sector' (Nutbrown 2013:45).

What this has meant in practice is an expectation, by the settings and education institutions, that students will behave and present themselves in a professional manner, both in the place of study and in their workplace or placement.

Students have expressed anxieties about what this 'professionalism' means for them, particularly if they are not qualified early years' practitioners and the sector is new to them. Consider the following question: What do settings expect of students? Write down some suggestions – for example, courtesy and appropriate dress. Why do these attributes matter?

However, professionalism is also about discrete standards and agreed ways of working; to be professional is to recognise external standards and desirable expectations and to be aware of how your authority and skills impact upon others.

You will already be making professional decisions in your early years' placement as well as your work placement (if different), so what does 'making professional decisions' mean for you?

Identify five contributory factors which enable or ensure that a professional decision has been made. You might think about negotiation or efficiency.

The important thing to note is that decision makers exercise power, and even if you feel, as a student-practitioner, that you make very few decisions, nevertheless you have, and do, exercise, power. Leeson (in Willan *et al.* 2007:173) recognises this issue of power and authority and cautions that the (practitioner's) personal attributes, attitudes and methods of engagement will inform people of their 'own self-worth and how, they in turn, could engage with others'. Respectful relationships, therefore, underpin professionalism and do much to remedy any imbalance of power.

Johnson (2010:49) reminds us that in the Early Years Foundation Stage one of the key principles is 'Positive Relationships' (DfE 2012:3) and notes, 'Respecting each other within every interaction (DCSF 2008b) is a challenge and is based on caring professional relationships.'

The DfES notes that professionalism is founded on respect and professionals should be 'self aware; know how to demonstrate a commitment to treating all people fairly; be respectful by using active listening and avoiding assumptions' (DfES 2005:9).

Furthermore, your colleagues may feel challenged by your developing knowledge and your access to knowledge that they feel, or know, they do not possess. Johnson (2010:28) invites us to think about 'affirmation' of our colleagues – that is, 'to express positive validation or assertion that someone or something is alright'.

Activity

Now reflect upon ways in which you have affirmed your colleagues, a parent or child. What did you do or say?

Briefly, then, how you treat colleagues, parents and children contributes to their understanding of themselves and this, in turn, impacts upon the people they meet and interact with.

So we can see why practitioners need to reflect in and upon practice as a lifelong professional commitment, allowing themselves to ask key questions about the influences that impact upon their practice. Failure to do so invites arrogance, ignorance and disrespect – the antithesis of professionalism.

Finally, then, Gould and Taylor (cited in Willan *et al.* 2007) identify further key reasons for reflection in practice; it reduces uncertainty, it enables competent transference of knowledge and skills to new or different situations and it generates creative, rather than programmed, responses.

The developing practitioner and the experienced practitioner also accrue benefits from reflection, achieving greater understanding of themselves and developing opportunities to work on their life scripts. It may help to resolve past conflict and develop new skills, knowledge and understanding.

Summary

You have begun to explore professionalism.
You have explored what contributes to a professional decision.
You have recognised that even as a student, you make professional decisions.
You have reflected upon issues of power and authority.
You have recognised how effective reflective practice may illuminate, modify or temper our professional approaches.

The developing practitioner in placement

Students owe an enormous debt of gratitude to the goodwill of early years' settings for their willingness to accept students of all persuasions. Nutbrown (2012:41) recognised that 'placements are an essential part of any early years student's training. These provide the opportunity to see and experience the realities of practice in settings.' Many students enjoy excellent experiences in nurseries, schools, day care centres and after-school clubs where colleagues are welcoming and helpful.

Others have less happy experiences; how you manage your setting experience will significantly impact upon your own learning and self-confidence. This section identifies some common student experiences and seeks to offer practical advice and activities to help you manage your own placement.

Audit: readiness for placement

You may well have received guidance earlier in your student journey, but it is good to reflect once again upon expectations.

These appear very basic, but they are the foundations of professional, courteous behaviour. Settings need to feel confident that you will dress appropriately, arrive at a specified time and turn up every week. If you are unable to achieve these basics, you will find your opportunities for professional development are negatively affected.

Audit: new placement

- Do you know where you are going? (Google Maps)
- Do you know how to get there? How long will it take?
- Do they have a dress code?
- Make a note of their address and phone number
- Carry some ID with you (e.g. student card)
- Do you know who to ask for on arrival?
- Is car parking available? If not, where do they recommend?
- Practice an introduction if you are not naturally confident – for example, 'Good morning. My name is Sue Bloggs, I am a student at . . . and I am on placement here every Friday . . .' (smile)
- If you are not given a health and safety, fire drill and security procedures overview, you should request one.

As a student you should never be held responsible for the effective management and instigation of health and safety procedures (unless you are employed there in a professional capacity), but it is your duty to be aware of them and know what to do in an emergency. Similarly, you are unlikely to be included in staff/ child ratios; however, the Early Years Foundation Stage guidance (DfE 2012:18) notes the following: 'Students on long term placements and volunteers (aged 17 or over) may be included if the provider is satisfied that they are competent and responsible.'

> There may be a named student mentor in the setting, whose role is to induct all students, oversee their time there and offer mentoring and support. Make notes as she/he talks to you and shows you round. Share any documentation you have been given by the placement coordinator on your course.

Once you have been welcomed, you will probably be allocated to a room or classroom and introduced to your room supervisor or class teacher.

As Yates with Appleby noted earlier in Chapter Three, arriving to a new classroom or room can be very unsettling; everyone knows what they are doing and you may feel like a spare part. If the age group is new to you, you may feel overwhelmed by the amount of movement and the range of activities. If it is a classroom with older children, it may feel quite formal and quiet.

Top tips

- Make yourself welcome by remembering to smile and show an immediate willingness to get involved with the children.
- A useful phrase is 'Where can I be useful?'
- If the setting is very different to your previous experience, use the observation skills you learnt as an emerging practitioner to help you see and understand what is happening.
- Make quick notes to help yourself – for example, 'The children ask each other for help before asking the teacher.' This helps you understand an ethos of peer support and independence, which prevails in the classroom.
- Listen to the language of adult-child interaction. It will be easier for you and the children if you show consistency.
- You will probably find you are very popular with the children! Use this popularity to learn names and a little bit about each child.
- Very young children may initially be wary of you, so be sensitive and respect their space.
- Be willing to help clear up, however menial the task. Offer – don't wait to be asked.
- Always say 'Thank you' before you leave.

What they don't always tell you, so you need to ask!

- Where to put your personal possessions – for example, bags.
- Where you can go for dinner break – for example, staffroom or other allocated space.
- Whether you should contribute to coffee/tea costs.
- Whether any children have a language, hearing or visual impairment which may affect communication.

Managing your academic work in placement

In her review, Nutbrown (2012:40) highlights that 'Education and caring for young children involves both theory and practice . . . (theoretical) knowledge needs to be supported by experience of working alongside experienced professionals.'

Most settings will be aware that you are a learner and that you will have academic assignments to achieve. It can, however, be difficult to find time to sit and discuss these with your teacher or supervisor and explain what you need to do. You are a guest in the setting; the staff may appear, and probably are, very busy, and it can be difficult to assert your needs.

Some practitioners will make it easy for you and ask if you have anything you need to do for your coursework.

You should respond positively:

- Share your module handbook or some part of it with your mentor. This helps him or her to understand what is expected of you;
- You should know when it has to be done. This is very important and will help your mentor plan with you;
- If you appear willing, your setting is more likely to be willing to help you.

A note about planning

The EYFS (DfE 2012:6) recommends a child-led provision. However, this involves ongoing planning, and in Key Stage 1 there is also a good deal of planning:

- Long-term planning
- Medium-term planning
- Weekly planning
- Personalised learning plans.

The point to remember is that your teacher or room supervisor will need to dovetail your assessment requirements with her planning. They will not welcome short notice. Many nurseries and day centres have ongoing programmes of visits, visitors and other agency support, so you need to plan ahead and share diaries.

Occasionally students experience reluctance on behalf of the setting to accommodate coursework and assessment tasks. You need to negotiate a friendly, non-threatening way forward. Reflect upon your own contribution: Are you willing and helpful, are you respectful and polite, do you make suggestions and show interest in the setting? Are you punctual and committed to excellent attendance?

If you are confident that you have achieved all of this, approach the supervisor again, thank her for her time and patience and ask for her help or advice – for example, 'I'd really appreciate your advice. I saw how well you did such and such and it reminded me about my assignment . . .'

This affirmation, as Johnson (2010) noted, supports respectful practice and open relationships. If this fails, arrange a meeting with your supervisor, take the module handbook with you and make it clear, politely, that the expectation comes from the university and you need the setting's support to achieve it.

Managing your professional development in your placement

Students occasionally report that they feel 'stuck' in their placement or that they are not offered opportunities to extend their experience – for example, they always hear children read, or they always get asked to wash up, mop up or wipe down after activities.

This is a difficult situation but one that needs addressing, and we shall look at how your academic work requirements may help you in this.

However, it is important to remember that even the most mundane and repetitive tasks are part of daily care and nurture in an early years' setting.

Practitioners may genuinely believe in a 'shop floor up' approach to learning in placement. Other practitioners may be glad to have another person in the room to help and not realize that you would enjoy the challenge of some other tasks as well.

What is clear, however, is that as a student-practitioner, you must take responsibility for your own learning and not depend upon anyone else to see to your needs (Burns & Sinfield 2008).

In your practice or professional development module, you may well be challenged to develop a personal development plan (PDP). There are other names, but basically it is about reviewing your development in key areas, identifying needs and identifying resources and opportunities. Keenan (cited in Burns & Sinfield 2008:301) likens a PDP to 'a set of building bricks on which to build your academic understanding, deepen your knowledge and understanding of yourself, and build your self-awareness and self-confidence'.

The world of postgraduate employment is increasingly interested in your 'soft skills', 'key skills' and 'employability skills' (Burns & Sinfield 2008) as well as evidence of your academic skills and abilities. To meet this demand, colleges and universities encourage students to reflect upon themselves in a holistic manner:

- Professional
- Academic
- Practice
- Some also encourage personal targets.

The important thing to remember is to make a PDP genuinely work for you, rather than as a paper exercise to achieve an assignment. Students who use it as a real tool to further their skills find it very encouraging to reflect, some months later, that all their targets were achieved and they can now look forward to setting new ones.

A PDP can be useful in placement to help you move forward in your development. You can identify in the PDP something that you would really like to do and, having embedded it in your PDP, approach the setting and ask if they can accommodate your aspirations because it is for college or university coursework. A good PDP arises from regular reflective practice which supports the practitioner in identifying realistic and relevant challenges.

Example of a simple professional development plan

In this instance the student had spent several weeks supporting activities in a Foundation Stage 2 (Reception) class, usually with reading or with worksheets for literacy. She felt that she was ready to negotiate planning an activity, but the teacher had been unforthcoming. During a tutorial, the student reflected upon why she felt she was ready to develop her skills and what was of particular interest to her, as Table 4.1 evidences.

Table 4.1 Case study using PDP to manage placement development, initial approach

Current Skill Level	Target level	Who can help me?	Evidenced	Time-line/Review
Clear, positive support with activities already available	To introduce an activity, using appropriate language of invitation, and participation	Class teacher Tutor	To introduce an activity for 5 children in the setting	End of half term

The student then used her PDP to help her identify her current skill levels and her challenge (target).

The first row of cells indicated her first manoeuvre: to approach the teacher with the PDP, which demonstrated that she needed to move on from working alongside the children, which she notes she does effectively, to introducing the activity. The student then presents her next step (second row).

This challenges her in presentation skills and language and social skills. The student reassures the teacher, through careful planning, that she is capable of this progression. Finally, having evidenced her ability to plan, provide and introduce an effective activity, the student plans her final step, which is to plan, provide and introduce a whole-class activity (see Tables 4.2 and 4.3).

Table 4.2 Case study using PDP to manage placement development, next steps

Effectively introduce an activity, its aims and objectives and initiate children's involvement	To plan and introduce an activity, with reference to EYFS planning and differentiation	Class teacher	To provide and introduce an activity for 5 children	End of term

Throughout the process, the student uses assignment expectations and requirements to clarify what she needs to do in placement: this gives legitimacy to her requests and reassures her placement supervisor that this is an appropriate development. This approach is also useful for students who may find aspects of practice quite intimidating.

Table 4.3 Case study using PDP to manage placement development, final target

Effectively plan and introduce an activity, with reference to EYFS and differentiation	To introduce a class activity, with reference to EYFS and differentiation	Class Teacher Teaching Assistant	To share planning with Teacher and Teaching Assistant and introduce class activity	End of half term

---

Case study

A student expressed her anxiety about approaching parents at the beginning and end of a session. She felt unsure of what to say and how to approach parents. We designed a PDP approach, which would validate the process for the setting but also provide her with incremental steps to achieve what was a challenging target for a shy person. See Tables 4.4 and 4.5.

Why is it important to gain confidence in talking to parents and carers?

Table 4.4 Case study 2 using PDP for placement challenges

Current skill level	Target skill level	Who can help me?	Evidenced	Review
Too nervous to approach parents	To speak to parents easily and confidently	?	Speaking to and greeting parents confidently	Half term

Here, the student is asking too much of herself in too short a time and seems unsure of who can help her. After some discussion in a tutorial, she devises a second PDP response.

Table 4.5 Case study 2 using PDP for placement challenges

Current skill level	Target skill level	Who can help me	Evidenced	Review
Not confident to approach parents at beginning and end of session	To talk to two parents each day at the end of the session	Colleagues; listen and watch them; note what they say and their manner	To record two instances of talking to parents	Half term

You can see how the target has been made smaller and more specific. The student still notes her lack of confidence and challenges herself to talk to two parents on her placement day. She chooses the end of the day because she feels she will be able to tell the parent something about the children – a common interest to share. The student-practitioner also recognises that observing her more experienced colleagues will provide tips and clues.

This brief case study shows you how usefully academic demands and reflective practice can be combined to help you move forward in placement. The student's discussion about her needs and how she met them, through the effective use of a PDP, may inform her reflective writing during her academic study.

Your PDP can also help you to move your academic work forward.

Planning your own journey

It is important to know what you hope for from your studying and your placement practice.

Activity

- Identify your current skills.
- Are they being used?
- Acknowledge your gifts and talents.
- Are they being used?
- Reflect upon what differences you note in yourself from when you first started studying (i.e. more confident, more focused).
- Reflect upon your placement and practice so far.
- Where do you want to be in five years' time?
- Have you made a start?

These reflections are important because they will keep you focused and positive. If you find any questions difficult to answer, then seek out a critical friend to help you in your reflective processes; this may be a colleague, a friend, a family member or a tutor. Higher education institutions will also have a strong career development presence on campus, which you may wish to access for further skills profiling and advice. The following questions may also help you:

- What have you learnt from your placement/workplace this year?
- Write down five things you know you are good at.
- Write down five skills you know (or people tell you) you have.

Activity

- Identify what changes you recognise in your professional journey.
- What are you doing differently now?
- What caused or prompted the changes?

We are each unique: no one else has the same mix of strengths, skills and personality as you. What you make of this potential is also up to you. The strength of reflective practice is that it provides you with opportunity to bring these threads together – professional, academic and personal – and achieve some synthesis. You will explore this notion of synthesis in greater depth as you progress through your studies.

When a placement isn't working

Most students benefit from useful, supportive and respectful placements during their academic study, and some go on to enjoy permanent employment at their study placement. However, there are occasions when the placement does not seem to work for you.

Before making a precipitous exit, you must ask yourself some key questions and be prepared to answer them honestly. Your tutor or academic supervisor may be able to support you in this.

Reflective questions

- Have you attended regularly?
- Have you been punctual and reliable?
- If you have been ill, have you kept in touch with the placement?

These are important basic questions because if you cannot confidently say 'yes' to any or all of them, then you have jeopardised your chances of a positive experience in this placement. The introduction of a 'key worker' for all children was enshrined in the Statutory Framework for Early Years Foundation Stage and highlights for all early years' practitioners the importance of relationships, continuity and security (DfE 2012). Therefore, if you are unreliable or unpunctual it suggests to the setting that you lack the professional commitment and understanding necessary for the role. In practice this means that they are unlikely to allocate you to a particular group, or take seriously any requests to participate beyond that of casual help.

Can you afford to leave now?

This is not a question about finances, although if you are an employee this will be a serious consideration and one that goes beyond the remit of this chapter.

Rather, it is for student-practitioners with academic work to complete, which may well require placement practice activity or insights. If you make a hasty or sudden exit, your college or university may not have, or be unwilling to offer, the flexibility to give you time to find another placement before handing in an assignment/assessment.

Ideally, you will contact your supervisor or tutor for discussion before making the decision to leave. If it is more expedient to remain at the placement, you will find some tips here to help make it survivable until a useful time to leave.

Surviving: Achieving an assessment outcome may help you to see the placement as a positive contributor to your success, rather than an obstacle to be avoided. Focus on the module handbook requirements to help you in relationships in the placement.

Is it the age group?

Just because you are studying the early years age group, it does not mean you will automatically enjoy all the age groups within it! For instance, I have over twenty-five years' experience across ages 3–7 years, but my first love is 3–4 year olds and then Year 1 (5–6 years). However, I can delight in all that babies are: the buoyancy and liveliness of toddlers and the confidence and independence of the seven-year-old. It is hugely important to know what comes before and what is possible beyond a preferred age group, so it is worth persevering. However, it may be the context or environment that you find difficult.

It may be helpful to consider these aspects:

- Are you more comfortable in an orderly, more predictable environment?
- Do you enjoy free-flow, flexibility and unpredictability?
- Do you feel more comfortable in larger groups or on a more intimate level with children?
- Do you feel happier being with the children all day or for a shorter time – for example, an after-school club?

Surviving: See the placement as part of a bigger picture. How will it help you to achieve your career aspirations? Set a key objective for each day and tick it when completed. This makes the placement more positive. Study the age range in a little more depth from key textbooks to help you anticipate and enjoy the children's activities.

Is it right for you?

Are you doing the studying that suits you best or are you conforming to what you feel is expected of you? Have you discovered that actually you don't want to work with children and their families? Are you feeling overwhelmed by work and study and your unhappiness at placement is symptomatic of wider issues? If any of these apply to you, they will negatively impact upon your commitment to and enjoyment of the placement. It is very important to talk to your tutor or supervisor or some other trusted person to find a way forward.

It is important to be confident of your choices because you will be investing a huge amount of time, energy and finance into the accomplishment of your academic course.

Surviving: Remind yourself that most students feel anxious, overwhelmed or insecure at some point in their studies. Seek support from university tutors or student support services. They are very experienced in supporting students, whereas friends and family may wish to immediately ease your unhappiness or discomfort and be less able, for all the best reasons, to see the longer-term view.

Is it the people/practitioners?

Sometimes students find themselves in settings that are themselves unhappy places to work. Staff may feel undervalued and underappreciated (Johnson 2010). They may feel under enormous pressure to achieve outcomes for the children. They may have more students than they can happily accommodate but feel unable to say so. While many settings offer a warm welcome and give generously to students of their time and expertise, some may appear uninterested in your progress or studying.

Where practitioners and other staff feel undervalued they may also be experiencing low self-esteem, which can manifest itself as aggression or hostility or indifference (Johnson 2010).

If you have persevered and reflected upon your own approach and contribution to your own satisfaction (page 73) it may be worth a conversation with your placement supervisor. This will be a delicate undertaking, and you will need to be sensitive in how you manage it.

Try saying, 'I would appreciate some feedback on my time here so far. I am feeling unsure about it and would value your insights.'

This allows time for them to reflect, consult with colleagues and make an appointment to provide you with feedback. It will also generate some interest in the setting because if they are asking other colleagues, they will become aware of this. You may find other practitioners ask if you are all right or if something is wrong. You need to think about what you will say. Again, avoid confrontation or blame. You could respond, 'I am grateful for everyone's help. I am just reflecting on my time here and will be glad of some helpful feedback.'

Surviving: Remember many students feel uncomfortable or insecure during placement; it is not always an issue of fault or failing. This sense of insecurity can sometimes affect how we see colleagues, rather than how they actually are. As before, see the placement as part of a journey to achieve your aspirations. Set a professional goal for each day, and remember to note its successful completion – for example, to thank someone specifically for his or her help. Offer to sort out a cupboard or tidy the staffroom. This gives you a sense of achievement, and a willing helper is hard to resist.

If, however, you feel that the placement is really not for you, then you need to manage your exit with courtesy and professionalism. You must inform your supervisor and also speak to the head teacher or manager as a matter of courtesy. If possible, time your departure to coincide with a holiday or semester change. You should also let your course tutor know, to avoid any possible embarrassment should he or she make a follow-up call to the setting to find out how you are progressing.

Consult with the supervisor about telling the children and parents. Your exit should never be so expeditious that you leave without anyone knowing that you are not returning. It is discourteous to the staff and unkind to the children. A letter of thanks is appropriate. A card may be acceptable, but choose with care and keep the message professional and simple.

Surviving: Keep to your decision once made. Do not avoid placement with unhelpful excuses. Speak professionally to and about the setting. Negative discussion is likely to reflect on you, not the setting. Identify what you have learned while there and how this can help you progress in your own development. Support your self-confidence and professional development by requesting time with your tutor to reflect upon the experience and plan ahead.

Remember

- These things happen.
- Leave with grace and courtesy; this is important for both your own self-confidence and for the setting's relationship with other students.

- Always write an expression of thanks – not an email and not just a telephone call.
- How you manage your exit will impact upon the setting's willingness to accept other students from your learning institution.
- It will also affect their view of the course or programme you are studying. We touched earlier on this notion of professionalism.
- Do not speak negatively of the setting in class; it is unprofessional and other students may be currently enjoying a placement there or looking forward to it.
- Move on! Learn from the experience by reflecting upon it.

Summary

This is a summary but not an end because what this chapter does not suggest is that the journey is complete; an exciting if daunting aspect of being a developing practitioner is that it is ongoing, as Moss (cited in Paige-Smith & Craft 2008:xvi) states: 'It (reflective practice) is a long and difficult journey, with no obvious end in sight but one that seems well-worth embarking upon.'

This chapter has suggested that to be a developing practitioner is to begin to acknowledge and experience practice on many different levels; in placement, in academic study and in reflection.

It has offered some theories of reflection which provide models upon which developing practitioners can build their reflective skills. We have recognised, in this chapter, that student-practitioners are increasingly seen as developing professionals and need to meet those challenges, through reflecting on issues of expertise, authority and power and how these impact upon relationships. We have briefly touched upon respect for children, parents and colleagues as being a crucial element in these relationships.

This chapter has recognised that the student-practitioner needs support to manage their placement effectively and has offered simple but effective strategies to help the student advance his or her skills base, both in placement and in study.

References and further reading

Burns, T. & Sinfield, S. (2008) *Essential Study Skills: The Complete Guide to Success at University*. 2nd ed. London: SAGE.

DfE (2012) *Statutory Framework for the Early Years Foundation Stage*. www.foundationyears.org.uk/early-years-foundation-stage-2012. Accessed 25/7/2013.

DfES (2005) *Common Core of Skills & Knowledge for the Children's Workforce*. Nottingham: DfES.

Farrell, P. (2010) *Early Years, Work Based Learning*. Exeter: Learning Matters.

Johnson, J. (2010) *Positive & Trusting Relationships with Children in Early Years Settings*. Exeter: Learning Matters.

Miller, L., Cable, C. & Goodliff, G. (2010) *Supporting Children's Learning in the Early Years*. London: Open University Press.

Nutbrown, C. (2013) *Foundations for Quality*. www.education.gov.uk/nutbrownreview. Accessed 24/7/2013.

Page, J., Clare, A. & Nutbrown, C. (2013) *Working with Babies and Children from Birth to Three*. London: Sage.

Paige-Smith, A. & Craft, A. (2008) *Developing Reflective Practice in the Early Years*. Berks: Open University Press.

Parker-Rees, R., Leeson, C., Willan, J. & Savage, J. (2010) *Early Childhood Studies*. 3rd ed. Exeter: Learning Matters.

Reed, M. & Canning, N. (2010) *Reflective Practice in the Early Years*. London: SAGE.

Sharman, C., Cross, W. & Vennis, D. (2004) *Observing Children*. 3rd ed. London: Continuum.

Willan, J., Parker-Rees, R. & Savage, J. (2010) *Early Childhood Studies* (2nd ed). Exeter: Learning Matters.

Chapter 5

The enabling practitioner

Christine Hey and Ruby Oates

By the end of this chapter you will:

- Understand what it means to be an enabling practitioner
- Understand what an enabling environment looks like
- Understand the importance of effective communication
- Understand the importance of positive relationships.

Introduction

This chapter builds upon the previous chapters and focuses on two key areas, the environment and communicating with others. We have found these aspects to be particularly important to the new student-practitioner as many of you enter higher education with limited experience of providing for, and relating to, young children. The first part of the chapter asks what an enabling environment may look like and what is an enabling practitioner. The second part of the chapter, in recognising the role of the student-practitioner within an enabling environment, explores the importance of effective interpersonal communication. It considers how an awareness of this supports the student-practitioner in learning how to communicate and relate positively to babies and young children.

What is an enabling environment?

'Every child deserves the best possible start in life and the support that enables them to fulfil their potential' (DfE 2012:2).

This introductory sentence to the Statutory Framework for the Early Years Foundation Stage assumes that users of the guidance will be able to recognise, and identify with, an enabling environment. Furthermore, it creates a distinction between a 'best possible start in life' and the support required to enable children to thrive.

However, practitioners may well argue that the two (best possible start and enabling support) must coexist, indeed, intertwine, if the child is to achieve his or her potential.

Activity

What constitutes a *'best possible start in life'*? (DfE 2012:2)
   Write down your suggestions as to what may contribute to this statement.
   Share with a colleague and discuss your findings; did you discover that a significant contribution was outside of the child – that is, dependent upon external influences – for example, home life, health and nutrition?

If this is the case then the role of the practitioner as an 'enabler' assumes huge significance in the life of the child. However, Oates (Chapter Seven) highlights how practitioners' expectations, qualifications and workplace environments affect how they see and fulfil their role. Practitioners work in a wide range of provision, meeting children and their families at different points in their lives when they may need individual and diverse facilities, support and provision. To become an enabling practitioner, requires us, then, to reflect on ourselves, the environments in which we work and the needs of the children who access our provision. Rather than attempting to immediately define what an enabling practitioner is, it may be useful to reflect, first, on what constitutes an enabling environment and position ourselves within it.

Page *et al.* (2013:109) recognise the interconnectedness of practice, provision and the practitioner in their discussion on creating environments for learning: 'before we really know children, when they first come into the setting and while we are getting to know them, we need to ensure the environment is such that it positively facilitates children's interactions, interests and involvement.'

To do this successfully, they suggest, the practitioner needs to have a thorough knowledge and understanding of children's development in order to anticipate the children's needs. This requirement for knowledgeable practitioners will be emphasised in more detail later.

Claxton and Carr (in Rose and Rogers 20132:126) note four types of environment as being useful in illuminating our understanding of the environments which are within the practitioner's power to create: 'A prohibiting environment, an affording environment, an inviting environment and a potentiating environment'.

Claxton and Carr (cited in Rose & Rogers 2012:126) identify a *'prohibiting environment'* as one that is tightly controlled by adults and schedules and fails to offer sustained activities. They suggest that this may include provision that offers *'carousel activities'* which are time-restricted and not respectful of children's learning patterns or styles.

An *'affording environment'* may be colloquially described as 'keeping the children occupied', but fails to challenge their thinking or further the children's learning opportunities. You may have visited one such provision, where practitioners observe but rarely get involved with the children's play or activities.

Claxton and Carr (cited in Rose & Rogers 2012:126) describe it thus: 'An inviting environment is one that not only affords the opportunity for learning but is one in which adults draw attention to its values and interests.'

Activity

In your own words describe an 'inviting environment'; what provision or images come to mind?

Finally, Claxton and Carr's fourth environment is described as 'potentiating' – that is, it identifies children's dispositions and actively stretches and develops them.

Reflect

What aspects of your practice do you find to be:

- Prohibiting
- Affording
- Inviting
- Potentiating.

Does it seem possible that 'prohibiting' may be appropriate in terms of health and safety?

The notion of the potentiating environment has, at its heart, a view of power and provision that places child and adult as equals in their participation; it is an environment that starts with the child, and is shared by the adult.

Eaude (2011:97) identifies two further descriptors: the inclusive environment and the notion of a 'hospitable space'. How do you think these two may differ or complement each other? Can an inclusive environment be anything less than hospitable? Could a hospitable environment actually exclude a child or his or her family?

The writer David Hare (cited in Eaude 2011:97) made a strong statement regarding his notion of a useful learning environment for children, when he said,

> . . . education has to be a mixture of haven and challenge. Reassurance of course. Stability. But also incentive. It's finding that balance. Finding it, keeping it . . . you care for them. You offer them security. You give them an environment where they feel they can grow. But you also make . . . sure you challenge them. . . . Because if you only make the safe haven, if it's all clap-happy and 'everything the kids do is great'. . . then what are you creating? Emotional toffees . . . who then have to go back and face the real world.

> **Activity**
>
> How do you feel about Hare's statement? Jot down some immediate responses. Reflect on any theoretical perspectives which may support or challenge the statement.

Providing an enabling environment

I mentioned earlier that, if we are to promote and provide an enabling environment which allows children to grow, to securely take on risk and challenge and to feel welcome, then we need to have, as a fundamental undertaking, a good knowledge of child development; there is insufficient space in this chapter to explore this in detail, but there is a wide range of resources which students can access to secure that knowledge, alongside their lectures and placement experiences.

However, briefly, we will explore what we know about how children learn, recognising individuality, influences, cultural experiences and the child's developmental stage(s). This knowledge should inform our practice and provision, resulting in an enabling environment which secures the best opportunities for children.

Eaude (2011) advises the practitioner to see learning as more than academic achievement, to recognise that learning is both individual and social and to reflect on process, not outcomes (this is challenging in the current political discourse, which focuses hugely on outcome and assessment; for a brief and unflinching recognition of the journey towards this current discourse, see Anning, in Moyles 2010).

There is, furthermore, a range of theoretical perspectives to assist our understanding, which you will meet during your studies. Palaiologou (2013) identifies several perspectives which may inform a practitioner's approach to providing an enabling environment.

Developmental perspective: This perspective arises from a biological and child development approach, which 'understand(s) development as a maturational process, taking place in different stages and ages' (Palaiologou 2013:58). Piaget was a key proponent of this approach; he identified a series of stages through which children journey, which he suggested display recognisable and universal cognitive attributes. While there are some anxieties about Piaget's research and claims, he did highlight the curiosity and inquisitiveness of young children. His research made a major contribution to our understanding that successful learning environments allow for exploration, questioning and experimentation.

Behavioural perspectives: These take the view that learning is a direct response to stimuli and external influences, through positive and negative feedback.

However, social learning behaviourists argue that 'Children are not passive in the learning process; instead their learning takes place within the social context and through observation, imitation, association and generalisation processes' (Bandura cited in Palaiologou 2013:59).

Furthermore, there is, now, recognition that the environments in which children live do impact upon their cognitive development; malnutrition, fear and poor early experiences impact negatively on young children, whereas stimulation and positive experiences increase a child's resilience and may ameliorate the negative impact of a poor start in life.

These child development perspectives helped to establish a view of childhood as a discrete period of life, during which children need particular and specific provision and nurture to enable them to flourish. These perspectives secured a view of children as developing in ages and stages and being curious and enquiring; thus, an enabling environment allowed for enquiry, exploration, stimulation and experimentation. Childhood was valued for itself, rather than as a precursor to adulthood, highlighted in practice by Montessori in her requirements for child-sized tools and furniture.

 Activity

Take some time to refresh your knowledge and understanding of the work of Piaget, Skinner, Froebel and Montessori.

Reflect on how their work still impacts upon early years' provision today.

Sociocultural perspectives: Palaiologou (2013:60) identifies the challenges that the sociocultural perspective offers to those discussed earlier. Vygotsky was a key figure in asserting that children do not learn in isolation (as suggested by Piaget's work), 'nor [are they] the product of direct stimuli of the environment and the process of positive or negative reinforcement argued by the behaviourists' (Palaiologou 2013:60).

Rather, sociocultural theorists argue that children are the product of a 'sociocultural milieu, its beliefs and values, and its customs and practices' (Vygotsky cited in Palaiologou 2013:60) – that is, they observe, participate, relate to and absorb that which is around them, of them and related to them.

One could counter this approach by asking whether children are ever a 'product', because they continue to develop, to learn, to assess and to reconsider into and throughout adulthood.

However, the notion of interdependency and the high status of relationships suggest that, to learn effectively, children utilise skills of problem solving, negotiation and making meaning. Vygotsky and Bruner further highlight the role of more knowledgeable 'others' (peers or adults) to facilitate these skills. Vygotsky (cited in Palaiologou 2013) proposed the notion of the Zone of Proximal Development – that is, the 'gap' between that which the child can successfully achieve independently and that which is possible with appropriate support. Bruner (cited in Palaiologou 2013) extended this notion, introducing the idea of 'scaffolding' – that is, how the more knowledgeable partner supports the learning in an appropriate and secure manner.

 Activity

Revise your knowledge and understanding of the work of Vygotsky and Bruner.

Reflect on placement activity; which perspectives are you currently employing in your work with children?

Make a note of your decisions in your reflective diary.

Furthermore, Palaiologou (2013) notes that Bronfenbrenner (1977) argued for a further, ecological theory which recognised the multifaceted nature of children's lives – that is, children live within systems, familial, communal and political. This theory suggests that no one aspect is more important than another, but rather it is the cumulative effect of all these systems that impacts upon the child.

Thus, a brief exploration of theoretical perspectives highlights how practitioners may adopt a view of childhood and how children learn, which will affect the environment they provide for the children in their care.

However, even as theory suggests that children do not operate in isolation, neither do practitioners; a further perspective arises from politics and policy, which we shall briefly explore. Baldock *et al.* (2012:1) are in no doubt about the weight of influence that others bring to bear on practice:

> We believe that the policies adopted by those in power make an enormous difference to the way practitioners are able to work. We also argue that policies are not just conjured up out of the air. People who make policies have reasons for what they do. We may not agree with them, but they are reasons, not mere whims. We need to understand those reasons in order to implement more effectively those policies that appear to be useful and to challenge more effectively those that do not.

Recent policies abound in the arenas of child protection, nutrition and health and, specifically, arising from the Statutory Framework for the Early Years Foundation Stage (EYFS) (DfE 2012). Policy brings with it a specific vocabulary; these may include targets, outcomes, stages and achievements. Policy may also change how we perceive the children in our care; not as a unique, successful being in that time and place, but as a future citizen, in whom key skills will be valued for their economic potential – for example, literacy and numeracy.

Furthermore, an emphasis on outcomes may lead to the construction of a deficit model of childhood – that is, the child is recognised not for his or her successes and competencies but rather for the areas in which he or she is perceived to be deficient. This may lead to an interventionist approach which seeks to rectify or ameliorate disability or disadvantage. However, others will argue that unless practitioners do address the delayed or struggling development, children are condemned to fall behind, with all that that entails in poor adult outcomes. For further reading, you will find Baldock *et al.* (2012) a thorough introduction to politics, policy and their impact on practice.

 Reflect

What is the language (vocabulary) used in assessment of children in your placement setting?

Make notes in your reflective diary of how children are described.

Finally, in our brief overview of perspectives, we address that of a rights perspective: the United Nations Convention on the Rights of the Child (UNCRC) (1989) established an important precedent in seeing children as 'citizens of today rather than individuals in the making' (Palaiologou 2013:63).

The UNCRC established children's rights to adequate living standards, health, education, rest and recreational activity, social security and participation in decision making in matters that affect them. This statement of entitlement provides governments with clear aims; those signatories to the UNCRC need to align their own policy to meet those established in the Convention. Palaiologou further notes that the revised EYFS is also positioned within a rights perspective as it requires practitioners to provide children with the best possible start to fulfil their potential.

Thus, we have come full circle to the beginning of this chapter, in establishing that theoretical perspectives, policy, practice and a rights agenda all inform the practitioner's response to the challenge of providing the best start in life for the children in his or her care. From here, we move into the enabling environment and what this means for children, practitioners and parents.

Aspects of an enabling environment

The revised version of the EYFS (DfE 2012) continues to recognise that the 'environment' is not just about internal and external landscapes but also incorporates a positive view of the child as a learner and the relationship between children and adults. Page *et al.* (2013:76) reflect on what this may mean for our youngest children:

> The revised EYFS (DfE2012a) summarizes the way in which adults should interpret how infants learn and develop by the presentation of an holistic view of the child and his learning and development. The formula:
> A Unique Child + Positive Relationships + Enabling Environment = Learning and Development

The physical spaces that we create for children, in which relationships are forged and learning experienced, are important, concerned as they must be with health and safety, access, functionality and invitation. It is important, as Page *et al.* (2013) note, to recognise the diversity of settings as they respond to community needs; for instance, the Pre-school Learning Alliance (www.pre-school.org.uk) arose from an active volunteer base using church and community halls to provide early years' provision, sometimes called 'pack away preschool'.

This may contrast sharply with a new, purpose-built early years' setting, or one housed in an old building with high windows and limited outdoor space. However, Page *et al.* (2013:121) caution against envy or assumption, noting that large spaces, breakout rooms and floor-to-ceiling windows may appear to parents and children as 'daunting, depersonalized and unfamiliar'. They finish with a critical statement, saying, 'After all, it is the relationships which are most important'. The central importance of communication and quality interactions will be discussed later in this chapter. Clark (2010), in her research into children's spaces, identified three overarching themes: participation, environments and relationships. You are very likely, as a student-practitioner, to be familiar with the latter two, but perhaps less aware of the growing interest in children as participants – that is, being involved in decision making, whether it is in day-to-day decisions or wider issues. This chapter does not allow time or space to thoroughly explore Clark's research, but further reading is recommended. However, Clark offers an interesting perspective on environments which is very relevant to this discussion:

> Early childhood spaces – whether these are nurseries, preschools or nursery classes within a school – are rich in symbols, rituals and routines. . . .Young children are engaged in everyday tasks such as meeting friends, having snacks, finding their pegs, playing on the bikes and listening to stories. It is a world of glue, toilet paper and sand. These objects and others define the day-to-day details of the young children's lives. It is also an environment in which the physical and emotional are bound together.
>
> (Clark 2010:12–13)

Thus, the physical environment, as part of a wider, holistic whole, matters to all concerned: parents, carers, children and practitioners.

At their most basic, enabling environments must provide a secure space for children; the Statutory Framework for the Early Years Foundation Stage (DfE 2012) makes very clear the requirements for settings, including childminders, day care nurseries attached to schools and reception classes.

> 3.53. Providers must ensure that their premises, including outdoor spaces, are fit for purpose. Spaces, furniture, equipment and toys must be safe for children to use and premises must be secure. Providers must keep premises and equipment clean and be aware of, and comply with, requirements of health and safety legislation (including hygiene requirements).
>
> (DfE 2012:23)

Activity

Take some time to read Section 3 of the EYFS (2012) and familiarise yourself with the requirements stated.

This concern for children's security, safety and well-being underpins the provision of an enabling environment. Functional activities like checking the garden or outdoor play spaces for glass, litter or animal faeces is a daily aspect of this ongoing care; sweeping up sand and paper clippings and mopping up spills is also part of this wider duty of care. Keeping the toilets clean and eating surfaces hygienic all adds to this notion of care which sometimes students find onerous; it is, however, essential.

Ensuring gates and fences are secure, equipment is safe and access systems not only work but also are observed by all setting users contributes to the children's welfare. When children, practitioners, carers and parents feel confident of the cleanliness and security of a setting, then relationships can thrive and learning prosper.

However, the notion of a 'Unique Child' (DfE 2012:2) – that is, 'Every child is a unique child who is constantly learning and can be resilient, capable, confident and self-assured' – reminds us that one size does not fit all; through observation, conversation and interaction, practitioners learn about each individual child, his or her needs and triumphs.

Furthermore, Gandini (in Featherstone 2011:32:32) stated the need for a flexible environment, which, anticipating Clark's work, incorporates and involves 'modification by the children and the teachers in order to remain up to date and responsive to their needs.'

We see again, then, the need for practitioners to be aware of child development and child behaviours and to be willing to observe and listen to the children, learning from the children what it is that they need to promote learning and engagement. Gould *et al.* (2012:11) believe that environments and spaces carry messages, to parents, children and practitioners; they suggest that 'Places speak to us and the children and practitioners get messages back from the children, including the things we hear them say and see them doing.' Furthermore, they claim that 'the learning environment is at the very heart of the early years' educator's practice, so much so that it feels almost fundamentally a reflection of the whole reason for ourselves and the children being there.'

Reflect

How do you feel about Gould *et al.*'s claim? If you agree, what importance does that give to the setting itself?

Reflect on your placement setting. How do you feel as you enter it?

Featherstone (2011), Goouch and Powell (2013), Clare (2012) and Hodgman (2011) all highlight the need for the environment to reflect and provide for the needs of the children; this means that a baby room will look significantly different from a preschoolers room or a reception classroom.

Activity

Identify what would make a physically enabling indoor environment from a crawling baby's viewpoint.

What would make a physically enabling indoor environment for a toddler? Is it different? How does it differ?

In the home setting, babies' and toddlers' needs must be met within a single environment; what can we learn from this?

Consider your placement setting; draw a floor plan and then consider in what ways it is enabling.

Clare (2012) offers challenging questions and reflections for practitioners regarding early years' provision and the assumptions that practitioners make about rooming by age, rather than by development. Using powerful case studies, Clare argues for a more flexible approach to transitions which respond to the child's development and needs, rather than to a rigid age routine.

Reflect

In your setting, is there flexibility in when children move to another room and if so, what informs that decision?

If not, what principles underpin a chronological transition policy?

Thus far we have considered the following:

- Enabling environments require practitioners to be knowledgeable about child development.
- Practitioners need to be aware that they may be working within a theoretical perspective of childhood and learning.
- Environments carry 'messages' to all who use them.
- An enabling environment is a safe, secure and clean environment.
- An enabling environment recognises each child's individuality and is flexible enough to respond to a child's needs.

Having, then, considered some key elements of an enabling environment, respectful of children's needs, suited to their development and safety, we move now to consider the practitioner who inhabits this environment, bringing to it a range of skills, attributes and dispositions.

What is an enabling practitioner?

The enabling practitioner, therefore, works within an environment that is safe, secure and respectful of and responsive to children's individuality. As Yates and Simmons (Chapter Eight) have also discussed, the enabling practitioner works with others, in teams, to promote an enabling environment for all, adults and children alike.

In an earlier chapter Yates with Appleby explored the title 'practitioner', its expectations and possible limitations within a context of a multilayered and multifaceted early years' sector. Currently, there are many descriptors for professionals who work with young children; teacher, practitioner, teaching assistant, classroom assistant, nursery nurse, nursery assistant, childminder and others (Nutkins *et al.* 2013). This plurality of roles has sometimes ill-served the early years' practitioner, with its various qualifications, expectations and employment terms and conditions added to the mix.

The Nutbrown Report (2013:5) highlighted the confusion around qualifications, roles, expectations and employment conditions, arguing for a more challenging, integrated and respectful approach to qualifications and employment for those who work with the youngest members of society: 'I am concerned that the current early years qualifications system is not systematically equipping practitioners with the knowledge, skills and understanding they need to give babies and young children high quality experiences.'

However, it is important to state that whatever the level of qualification, salary and working conditions, many practitioners bring to their practice a range of positive intentions and skills to support and care for children. Nutbrown (2013:16) recognised this in her summary: 'Those many practitioners who took the time to contact me were proud of their work and passionate about the quality experiences they offered to young children.'

Nutbrown identified several key points which she argued are central to quality practice and which impact upon every student-practitioner (2013:21–23); these include a thorough understanding of early language development, a sound understanding of special educational needs and disability, an understanding of the importance of play and an awareness of the underpinning importance of observation and assessment in planning and providing appropriate experiences for young children. Furthermore, awareness of teamwork and the opportunity to study are also highlighted.

 Activity

Identify the modules you have studied, or are currently studying, which will help you to achieve these desirable outcomes as a practitioner.

So, a brief exploration of current discussion and debate has highlighted not only the need for enabling environments but also the central role that the practitioner plays in achieving these.

Aspects of an enabling practitioner

It could be suggested that an enabling practitioner brings skills, attributes and dispositions to the care and education of children. A skill can be taught, acquired, secured and refined – for example, driving a car or learning to knit. An attribute is a quality or property – for example, play dough is malleable and pliant; these are its attributes. A disposition can be described as a personality or behavioural tendency.

So, enabling practitioners may be utilising their personality, their qualities and their acquired skills.

In Table 5.1, identify a range of skills, attributes and dispositions which you believe support effective work with children.

Table 5.1 Personal audit

Skills	Attributes	Dispositions
Secure and accurate knowledge of child development	Hard-working	Patient

In the chapters 'The Emerging Practitioner', 'The Developing Practitioner' and 'The Critically Reflective Practitioner', you are challenged to reflect upon your practice, to ensure that you maintain professionalism, criticality, competence, creativity and flexibility. Looking at your responses in the foregoing activity, reflect on what may be the potential dangers of over-relying on any one aspect.

Having acknowledged the importance of an enabling environment and their individual competencies and personality, enabling practitioners discover that a wide range of roles and expectations await them in the setting.

Rose and Rogers (2012:2–3) identify what they call 'seven selves' of the practitioner: 'The Critical Reflector, the Carer, the Communicator, the Facilitator, the Observer, the Assessor, the Creator'.

It is interesting to note how and why Rose and Rogers (2013:3) identified these 'plural practitioners'; they explain that 'The notion of the plural practitioner came about as a result of many comments by student practitioners that they had to be a different person depending on what they were doing at the time.'

 Activity

Identify any events or occurrences when you accessed these 'seven selves' identified by Rose and Rogers (2013).

Do you share the same understanding of what each 'self' means?

Discuss how your current skill levels supported you in these experiences and when you felt you drew on your own personality and disposition.

The enabling practitioner recognises each child as an individual and each family as a unit with its own concerns and expectations, experiences and aspirations.

Jot down what skills and attributes will help you to be responsive to each child.

Make further notes on what skills and attributes will help you to support individual families and their members. You may find you have written down sensitivity, knowledge, confidentiality, time, patience, kindness and respect, among others. Can you see, however, how our own personality is not necessarily the most important part of these interactions, but rather it is locating *within ourselves*, regardless of whether it is familiar and comfortable, what is the best response to each individual, whether they are colleagues, children, carers or parents.

We may not naturally be good listeners, but we can learn *how* to listen and become sensitive to when and where to listen to those we work with and alongside.

We may find it hard to empathise with a situation we have not experienced, but nevertheless, by listening carefully, observing and being patient, we may secure enough understanding to ensure our response is appropriate and supportive.

We may be very gregarious and extrovert, but we learn to pause, to sit alongside but not overwhelm the youngest or shy child in our setting. An enabling practitioner recognises that his or her 'self' may need to adapt, moderate, expand or challenge to meet the needs of children. For further exploration, you could read Carl Rogers's contribution to our understanding of self-esteem and the notion of 'unconditional positive regard' when working with others; see Rogers (1961) and, for an introduction, see Doherty and Hughes (2009:387).

Activity

Identify an enabling practitioner from a child's point of view – for example, fun and caring.

Identify an enabling practitioner from a carer or parent's point of view – for example, competent and safe.

Identify an enabling practitioner from a colleague's point of view – for example, reliable and knowledgeable.

We have, so far, explored how different child development theories may affect our approaches to young children, recognised that young children attend a variety of provision, in different buildings and for different reasons, influenced by policy and politics; we will now consider the central importance of communication and interaction which makes early years' provision a fertile place for children's social, emotional and cognitive development.

The enabling practitioner: effective communication and the development of positive relationships with babies and young children

In Chapter Three, Yates with Appleby note that two key attributes are fundamental to all early childhood education and care settings; these are team working and working in relationship with others. In Chapter Four, Hey's Top Tips reminds the student-practitioner of the importance of effective communication and appropriate interpersonal skills when first entering the placement setting. Here we explore the importance of effective communication and how students can develop their skills and understanding to promote positive relationships with babies and young children. It is important to remember that no matter how shy you are as a person, communication skills can be improved and developed, leading to a confident and engaging student-practitioner who forms successful relationships with young children and the adults in the placement setting.

What is communication?

Throughout all our lives we communicate with others so much so that we often never stop and think about what is actually involved; it comes second nature to most of us, but how do we define communication? Petrie (2011:18) says,

Communication takes place when someone sends a message and the other person receives it. It is a two-way process. You play your part in the communication by listening and to being attentive to other people, as well as by talking to them.

Communication is much more than speaking clearly and fluently, though that in itself is very important to you as a student-practitioner. Communication is also non-verbal, including signs and symbols, the use of space, body language and facial expression, eye contact and tone of voice. The social psychologist Michael Argyle (1994) highlights the importance of non-verbal behaviour and suggests that up to 93 per cent of messages can be attributed to non-verbal communication (NVC). Doherty and Hughes (2009) suggest that Graddol *et al.*'s (1994) six features of NVC are still accepted as a useful guide; these include gesture, body contact, posture, proxemics (personal space), gaze and facial expressions. (For further reading, see Doherty & Hughes 2009).

Paralanguage, or wordless sounds, includes sounds but not words with literal meanings – for example, when we respond to others through a grunt or a huff. We have a shared understanding of this because wordless sounds are utilised regularly in our own language, locality, region and culture. Wordless sounds are particularly meaningful to you as a student-practitioner because babies and young children convey meaning through many different types of wordless sounds, such as squealing, yawning, crying and laughing.

 Activity: verbal and non-verbal communication between adults and young children

- When undertaking placement observations as part of your course, include an aim that incorporates an observation of social interactions between adults and babies and/or young children.
- Pay particular attention to the utilisation of space, facial expression, body language, touch, signs, wordless sounds, eye level and height to suit children's individual needs.
- Note also the different aspects of speech as such as tone of voice, pitch and pace as well as the words spoken.
- Note how different forms and types of communication and social interaction used by the adults determine different responses from babies and children.
- In an ethical manner, write up your findings in your reflective diary and evaluate what you learned about social interaction with babies and/or young children.

Crow *et al.* (2008:7) note that communication with young children can involve touching, listening, the tone of your voice, gestures, playing, observing, signing, explaining, receiving and transmitting information as well as interpreting and reflecting. When we communicate with one another, we draw upon our own theoretical knowledge, cultural understandings and lived experiences as a person of a particular gender, ethnicity, age, disability, culture, belief, faith, socio-economic status, locality, region and geography.

Activity: cultural differences in social interaction in the early years

- Conduct a literature search of early childhood academic journals to find three articles on different cultural models of teacher-child interaction in the early years setting. A useful example is Jingbo and Elicker (2005) on the Chinese kindergarten.
- Consider how the findings and ideas presented in the three articles have widened your understanding of the different ways in which we communicate and interact with one another across the world.

Ineffective communication can have many negative consequences, so it is important for you as the student-practitioner to be professionally effective in the ways in which you interact with others in the placement setting. This includes babies, young children, parents, your placement supervisor and other professionals. From our experience, most of the problems arising from work experience relate to a lack of confidence and skills on the part of the student-practitioner to communicate clearly and regularly with his or her supervisors and other professionals. Crow *et al.* (2008:7) recognise the importance of communication, noting, 'When done badly it can be confusing, discriminatory, alienating, deflating, cause harm or create problems.' When done well, it builds positive relationships and supports children's learning and development, making a significant contribution to their well-being. As importantly, Crow *et al.* (2008) note, effective communication skills have the potential to empower children, keep them safe, affirm their identity and encourage their creativity.

Degotardi *et al.* (2013:5) note Hendrick's (2004) ideas about how children are, in the main, involved in two types of relationships in the early childhood setting: 'the child-teacher relationship and peer relationship – and these different relations serve distinct, overlapping and complementary functions for the child.' The child-teacher relations, they note, provide children with emotional security, protection, nurturance and care. While in the child-peer relationship, children are seen to care for others, assist, protect and provide emotional support to their peers (for more, see Degotardi *et al.* 2013).

Activity: the potential of effective communication skills

Provide an example of how effective communication skills in the placement setting can:

- Empower children
- Keep them safe
- Affirm their identity
- Encourage their creativity.

Petrie (2011) reminds us of the importance of verbal and non-verbal interpersonal communication because of the key part it plays in the development of positive relationships with children. Learning how to develop positive relationships with children and adults is a key skill in working in the early years' setting.

What is social pedagogy and why is it important to our social interactions with young children?

Petrie (2011) notes that forming relationships is the central process in working with children and is first and foremost personal. She suggests that the most effective ways of communicating with young children are underpinned by a social pedagogical approach. Social pedagogy, she explains, is

> where care and education meet, relating to support for children's development, overall. To put it another way, social pedagogy is about bringing up children, it is 'education' in the broadest sense of that word and is concerned with the whole child: a physical, thinking, feeling, creative human being, in relationship with other people and already contributing to our society.
>
> (Petrie 2011:7)

Petrie says that social pedagogy is based on values and not on techniques; it is a form of ethical childcare practice that is underpinned by values that demonstrate respect for adults and children in equal measure. Petrie suggests that social pedagogy, as a professional occupation, requires social pedagogues (the practitioners) to possess certain professional understandings, attitudes and skills before they can involve themselves in bringing up children as a whole person. See Yates with Appleby, and Hey in earlier chapters, taking account of their discussions about children's holistic development.

Dalli (cited in Miller & Cable 2012) suggests that social pedagogy recognises and values the place children have in society in terms of how we communicate and relate to them. It must include being knowledgeable about children and contemporary research and theories about early childhood, as a starting point for professional practice and critical reflection. It also means working together with colleagues and children by being respectful, supportive and working in partnership with them. For a discussion about relational pedagogy and early childhood studies students, see Oates and Sanders (2009).

Emilson and Folkesson (2006:236) in their research findings note the importance of the teacher being 'emotionally present' in the activities. The teacher should be observant and confirming and 'tune in' with the children (Emilson & Folkesson 2006:236) in order to develop a free dialogue.

Activity: understanding social pedagogy

- Using an academic early childhood journal, find an article that provides you with an understanding of social pedagogy and the role of the pedagogue, summarising the key points.
- Discuss your understanding of it with your tutors and peers either at a tutorial or in class. Consider what aspects of your placement setting you perceive as using elements of social pedagogy.

Why is effective communication important for the young child's development?

As a student of early childhood studies you will, through your early language and communication, emotional and social development modules, already appreciate how important interpersonal communication and reciprocity are in the development of babies and young children's bonding and attachment relationships with significant others. Foley and Leverett (2008:11) suggest that communication is fundamental to children's development and it is one of the ways in which children develop cognitively, socially and emotionally. They state, 'Children need communication to develop their own communication skills and their understanding of their society and culture.' (For further reading, see Foley & Leverett 2008.) They note that the first dyadic relationships – that is, those between caregiver and child, usually the biological parents – are the building block for connections in the brain. Foley and Leverett (2008:11) state that

> Soothing communications help build self-soothing skills, consistent communication patterns help build an understanding of cause and effect, early exposure to child-direct language lays the foundation for developing language, empathic response helps the child understand their own and others' emotions.

Canning (2011:52) notes the significant contributions of Bowlby (1988), Trevarthen (2005), Ainsworth (1969) and Winnicott (1971) in helping us appreciate the importance of the infant's social interaction with others, noting, 'Children are driven to build relationships and are able to communicate and form reciprocal bonds from a very young age.' For further reading see also Brock and Rankin (2008).

Clare (2012:26) also notes how the emotional expressions of caregivers help lay the foundations of babies and young children's emotional development. In the nursery setting, this is a means of establishing a relationship between the practitioner and the baby. Clare (2012:31) argues, 'Perhaps if we left our children to become emotionally secure before introducing an academic curriculum, then fewer of our children would become disaffected as they progress through our current target-led education system.' For more in-depth reading on working with children from birth to three years, please see Clare (2012) and Page et al. (2013).

Activity: tools to measure children's well-being and involvement

- Conduct a literature search to find out about the use of assessment tools to measure children's well-being and involvement in the early years' setting.
- Note how such tools are used to assess babies and young children's levels of well-being and involvement in the nursery setting.
- In what ways do such tools benefit young children and what are their limitations?

Communication and social interaction are equally important to babies and children's cognitive development, as you know from your readings of Piaget, Bruner and Vygotsky in your early childhood studies modules. These writers noted the importance of the environment and the child's interaction with the adult to co-construct his or her learning. Smidt (2009:139), in her guide to Vygotsky, notes that all learning is social: 'Social, in this sense, refers to more than the presence of others. It refers to the previous experiences of the learner and the use of socially and culturally constructed tools.'

> The importance of the early communication environment in a child's first two years of life is a key finding in a research report by Roulstone *et al.* (2011:39), who note the implication of their findings for practice: The provision of language rich environments within early years provision is certainly a necessary condition for good outcomes, carrying with it implications for the training of the children's workforce who must provide these enabling communication environments and also work with parents to do the same in the child's home context.

A key message from their findings (see Roulstone *et al.* 2011:40) is that the context in which children learn in their youngest years is of critical important to their transition into the education system.

While communication plays an important role in children's cognitive development, it plays an equally important role in the development of their social and emotional well-being. Foley and Leverett (2008), in noting the importance of communication in children's social and emotional development, suggest the prioritising of children's social and emotional literacy. Through this, children are supported in the development of their emotional literacy, enabling them to recognise their feelings, manage and recognise their own emotions and those of others, and be able to talk about their feelings.

Activity: children's emotional literacy

- As a student-practitioner, find out in an appropriate, sensitive and ethical manner your placement setting's strategies towards responding to children's expressions of emotion and how these support the development of children's emotional literacy.
- Discuss with your placement supervisor how you, as a student-practitioner, can develop an understanding of the ways in which children's emotional literacy is developed through activities and approaches in the setting.
- In your reflective diary consider in an ethical manner the ways in which children's emotional literacy is developed and how the setting responds to children's expressions of emotion in the setting.

A further reason why communication is important in the early childhood setting relates to the rights of children to express their views and participate fully within it. Winter (2011) suggests that a child rights approach is necessary in social workers' work so that they can see beyond the child as a 'case'. In noting the United Nations

Convention on the Rights of the Child (UNCRC), Winter (2011:58) states, 'The UNCRC views children as individuals entitled to a range of basic rights and freedoms and as active contributors exercising these rights within the context of their families and communities.' She notes the recent UN best practice principles for working with children (for more see Winter 2011) and how these principles must underpin relations and communication with young children.

Activity: the rights of the child to be heard

Access the OHCHR (2009) Committee on the Rights of the Child via the link in the References section of this chapter.

- Access Comment No. 12, 'The right of the child to be heard' through this link. Please read the whole document.
- Pay particular attention to Section C4, 'In Education and School'.
- Consider the ways in which childcare settings can adhere to the principles in Section C4, and discuss what barriers might exist to their implementation.

Bae (2009) draws attention to how Norway has embraced children's participation in the kindergarten through the provision of a kindergarten act followed by a Framework Plan (NMoER 2006), which contains national guidelines for all Norwegian kindergartens with regard to children's participation. (For the most recent framework document see NMoER 2012.) Bae (2009:393) notes that this includes children being able to express themselves through various modes and a requirement that staff listen to children and attempt to interpret their body language. (For a recent review see the Norwegian Ministry of Children & Equality 2008.) Within the Norwegian tradition in early childhood settings democracy is recognised as a value, thus ensuring that children actively participate in the setting and in a democratic society. For an interesting discussion on preschool teachers' language use in Norway, and how it invites children to participate in democratic conversation, see Tholin and Jansen (2012).

Developing effective interpersonal communication skills in the practice setting

Ethical practice

Petrie (2011) reminds us that social pedagogy is an ethical practice, and throughout this textbook, the authors have reminded you as the student-practitioner about how to conduct yourself in an ethical manner in the placement setting, particularly in relation to conducting observations in your placement. Working from an ethical standpoint should underpin all your actions when communicating and interacting with others; this includes handling information with care and sensitivity. Information could come to you in different ways – for example, overhearing a conversation, or a parent confiding in you. An important part of ethical practice is being trustworthy, and as Petrie (2011) notes, when someone discloses private information about a child or family it is extremely important that you do not disclose it to others and gossip about it. The consequences of such disclosure can be hurtful and harmful. For university students on placement, such behaviour can lead to exclusion from the placement and disciplinary procedures being instigated by their university.

When someone, parents or colleagues, discloses private information about children and families, obviously you should not gossip about it. It takes little imagination to understand how hurtful it would be for your own private business to be discussed by other people, and so you extend the same respect to others.

As Yates with Appleby, and Hey note in earlier chapters, as a student-practitioner, you should think of yourself as a professional and behave in a professional and ethical manner at all times. If you are invited to attend a meeting about a child, it is important that you recognise this is a compliment to the trust in which you are held. (For an excellent discussion on how to convey respect for others and avoid disrespect, see chapter 9 of Petrie 2011.) Furthermore, in recognising that all of us have differing individual needs, you, as a future professional working with young children, have a responsibility to seek out opportunities to develop your understanding of alternative forms of communication. This should include knowledge and skills that support your social interaction with all children, including those who have additional needs – for example, finding out about the role technology now plays in supporting communications, and learning a sign language.

Effective speaking, listening and responding

For the student-practitioner the skills and confidence related to effectively speaking, listening and responding to young children take time to develop. There are, however, skills you can use to develop your confidence in interacting with others; it is important you recognise the value of being a dialogic practitioner who is willing to engage in conversation in the setting. Durden and Rainer Dangel (2008) suggest there are a number of ways practitioners can develop their communication skills with young people. The task in Table 5.2 includes some of their ideas to help you think about how you can improve your communication skills with young children.

Table 5.2 Developing your speaking, listening and responding skills

Useful skills:	Provide an example of how you could do this:
Ask how and why questions.	
Use language to challenge children cognitively.	
Make connections to children's experiences.	
Encourage children to become conversational partners.	
Structure and guide activities that facilitate children's language and thinking.	
Use purposeful and open-ended activities to promote children's conversational skills.	

Developing effective communication skills
for working with young children

Another important aspect of communication is listening to others. Listening means not only hearing a voice but also using your developing observational skills to consider how the person is communicating with you. People convey meaning through their non-verbal communication (NVC), so the skilled listener is able to evaluate how the verbal and non-verbal messages contradict or support one another.

Listening and observing are particularly important when relating to babies and very young children. Petrie (2011) reminds us that babies use a range of signals to draw adults into communicating with them, such as appearance, crying, smiling and imitating; therefore, careful listening and observing are essential skills for those who work with others, including babies and young children. For more on communicating with babies in particular, please see Page *et al.* (2013) and Goouch and Powell (2013).

Petrie (2011) suggests that careful listening involves:

- Hearing and attending to what the other person is saying.
- Demonstrating respect for what is being said by not interfering.
- Allowing the person time to speak at his or her pace and ability.
- Being sensitive, patient and responsive.
- Finding ways to understand one another – for example, asking for an interpreter.
- Finding ways to support the speaker to enable him or her to speak.
- Avoiding environmental distractions and interruptions.
- Using NVC messages to encourage interaction.
- Using reflective feedback to check that you have understood the message.

Activity: listening and attending

- In pairs, each individual has three minutes to speak about his or her interests and ambitions. When it is your turn to listen, use the ideas provided by Petrie (2011) to develop your skills as a careful listener. Afterwards provide feedback to the speaker by checking out with him or her what he or she said.

- In the placement setting, observe the ways in which professionals use the foregoing techniques to demonstrate careful listening. In an ethical manner, record in your journal what techniques and behaviours you found effective.

McSporran, writing in 1997, lamented the poor quality of many teaching and learning environments in relation to environmental acoustics and background noise. Listening, therefore, is about you as a practitioner listening and hearing what a child is communicating; it means ensuring that a child can hear you. McSporran (1997:18) says, 'There is a clear need for a change in attitude to promote a culture of optimising the listening and learning environment from the start of the educational process.'

While listening skills play a key role in successful interactions with children, talking with children can present some difficulties for the inexperienced student-practitioner. Egan (2009) notes the development of good questioning skills is a key focus for many students, and they must recognise that questioning involves a range of skills and that different skills are likely to foster different outcomes. Effective questioning skills take time to develop, and it is useful for you, as a student-practitioner, to observe how experienced and expert practitioners enable children to engage in rich conversations with them. Gjems's (2010) research found children very eager to engage and participate in conversations with the teacher. She argues that early childhood teachers should have extensive knowledge of the different ways to ask open-ended questions and 'how they can invite children to narrate and share their thoughts' (Gjems 2010:147). For the student-practitioner such as yourself, it is important to remember that open-ended and prefaced questions (see Gjems 2010:144 for examples) using the interrogative 'what' are useful in engaging children in conversation. For an interesting discussion on the use of question posing with children see Chappell et al. (2008).

 Activity: developing your questioning skills

- Experiment with using 'what', 'how' and 'why' questions when next in the placement setting.
- If you have an opportunity to undertake some small group work with children, practise using open-ended questions.
- In an ethical manner, review in your reflective diary the use of open-ended questions.

For an interesting discussion on the quality of the child and adult interaction in early years' settings in the Netherlands, see the research findings in de Roos et al. (2010).

Responding and giving feedback

Petrie (2011:61) suggests that the caring, careful listener is also able to provide feedback in a positive way in the form of encouraging sounds, nods, smiles and words (for more see Petrie 2011). In this way, you demonstrate that you are interested in what the person has to say. You are then much more likely to elicit a positive response from him or her and therefore build positive relationships. She says that reflecting back is a special form of feedback that can be very useful to let someone know that you have heard and understood him or her:

Reflecting back is when you repeat to the speaker the main things he or she has just said; it is as though you are a mirror. Although this sounds as though the other person might find what you say boring, in the right circumstances people welcome reflecting back as a demonstration that you have really heard and understood them. (Petrie 2011:65)

 Activity: checking out you have understood the message

- Practise your 'reflection back' (Petri 2011:65) skill in university by checking out with a module tutor if you have understood (a) the assessment task and (b) the assessment criteria of a particular piece of coursework.
- As Hey suggests, practise your reflecting back skills by asking your placement supervisor for verbal feedback on your progress to date.
- Having received this feedback, check out with your supervisor that you have fully understood it through a process of reflecting back.
- Review how you can utilise reflecting back skills when communicating with young children in the practice setting. Following ethical guidelines, record in your reflective diary your progress, evaluating what worked well and what did not.

Chapter summary

This chapter gathers together some key threads for the student-practitioner, which apply not only to the novice student but also to the experienced practitioner student. You are reminded that settings vary but the children's needs remain central; furthermore, you are invited to recognise the influence and impact of policy and sector changes and to secure for yourself a thorough grounding in child development to enable you to provide children with an informed provision that challenges negative influence and enhances positive policies.

You are invited to consider the purpose and meaning of an enabling environment in which you, as the practitioner, remain central to providing a place in which children thrive. This is a practitioner who is respectful, ethical and articulate with effective communication skills underpinned by critical thinking, a strong knowledge base and a sound understanding and appreciation of relational pedagogy.

References and further reading

Ainsworth, M. (1969) 'Object Relations, Dependency and Attachment: A Theoretical Review of the Infant Mother Relationship.' *Child Development* 40 (4): 969–1025.

Argyle, M. (1994) *The Psychology of Interpersonal Behaviour*. London: Penguin Group.

Bae, B. (2009) 'Children's Right to Participate – Challenges in Everyday Interactions.' *European Early Childhood Education Research Journal* 7(3): 391–406. http://dx.doi.org/10.1080/13502930903101594 (accessed 24 July 2013).

Baldock, P., Fitzgerald, D. & Kay, J. (2012) *Understanding Early Years Policy*. 3rd ed. London: SAGE.

Bowlby, J. (1988) *A Secure Base*. London: Routledge.

Brock, C. & Rankin, A. (2008) *Communication, Language and Literacy from Birth to Five.* London: SAGE.

Bruce, T. (2004) *Developing Learning in Early Childhood.* London: Paul Chapman.

Canning, N. (Ed) (2011) *Play and Practice in the Early Years Foundation Stage.* London: SAGE.

Chappell, K., Craft, A., Burnard, P. & Cremin, T. (2008) 'Question-Posing and Question-Responding: The Heat of "Possibility Thinking" in the Early Years.' *Early Years: An International Research Journal* 28(3): 267–286. http://dx.doi.org/10.1080/09575140802224477 (accessed 23 July 2013).

Clare, A. (2012) *Creating a Learning Environment for Babies and Toddlers.* London: SAGE.

Clark, A. (2010) *Transforming Children's Spaces: Children's and Adult's Participation in Designing Learning Environments.* Oxon: Routledge.

Crow, G., Foley, P. & Leverett, S. (2008) 'Communicating with Children.' In P. Foley & Stephen Leverett (eds), *Connecting with Children: Developing Working Relationships.* Bristol: Policy Press in association with The Open University.

Degotardi, S., Sweller, N. & Pearson, E. (2013) 'Why Relationships Matter: Parent and Early Childhood Teacher Perspectives about the Provisions Afforded by Young Children's Relationships.' *International Journal of Early Years Education.* http://dx.doi.org/10.1080/09669760.2013.771325 (accessed 25 June 2013).

Demuth, C., Keller, H. & Yovsi, R.D. (2012) 'Cultural Models in Communication with Infants: Lessons from Kikalkelaki, Cameroon and Muenster, Germany.' *Journal of Early Childhood Research* 10(1): 70–87. http://dx.doi.org/10.1177/1476718X11403993 (accessed 23 July 2013).

de Roos, S.A., van der Heijden, M.R.H.M. & Gorter, R.J. (2010) *European Early Childhood Education Research Journal.* http://dx.doi.org/10.1080/13502930903520017 (accessed 23 July 2013).

DfE (2012) *Statutory Framework for the Early Years Foundation Stage.* www.foundationyears. org.uk/early-years-foundation-stage-2012 (accessed 29 July 2013).

DfE (2013) *Development Matters in the Early Years Foundation Stage (EYFS).* www. foundationyears.org.uk/wp-content/uploads/2012/03/Development-Matters-FINAL-PRINT-AMENDED.pdf (accessed 15 January 2014).

Doherty, J. & Hughes, M. (2009) *Child Development: Theory and Practice 0–11.* Harlow: Pearson Education.

Durden, T. & Rainer Dangel, J. (2008) 'Teacher-Involved Conversations with Young Children during Small Group Activity.' *Early Years: An International Research Journal* 28 (3): 251–266. http://dx.doi.org/10.1080/09575140802393793 (accessed 23 July 2013).

Eaude, T. (2011) *Thinking through Pedagogy for Primary and Early Years.* Exeter: Learning Matters.

Egan, B. (2009) 'Learning Conversations and Listening Pedagogy: The Relationship in Student Teachers' Developing Professional Identities.' *European Early Childhood Education Research Journal* 17 (1): 43–56. http://dx.doi.org/10.1080/13502930802689012 (accessed 23 July 2013).

Emilson, A. & Folkesson, A-M. (2006) 'Children's Participation and Teacher Control.' *Early Child Development and Care* 176 (3–4): 219–238. http://dx.doi.org/10.1080/03004430500039846 (accessed 23 July 2013).

Featherstone, S. (2011) *Setting the Scene: Creating Successful Environments for Babies and Young Children.* London: A & C Black.

Foley, P. & Leverett, S. (Eds) (2008) *Connecting with Children: Developing Working Relationships.* Bristol: Polity Press in association with The Open University.

Gjems, L. (2010) 'Teachers Talking to Young Children: Invitations to Negotiate Meaning in Everyday Conversations.' *European Early Childhood Education Research Journal* 18 (2): 139–148. http://dx.doi.org/10.1080/13502931003784479 (accessed 25 July 2013).

Goouch, K. & Powell, S. (2013) *The Baby Room: Principles, Policy and Practice*. Berks: Open University Press.

Gould, T., Brierley, J. & Coates-Mohammed, K. (2012) *Learning and Playing Indoors: How to Create an Inspiring Indoor Environment*. London: Bloomsbury.

Graddol, D., Cheshire, J. & Swann, J. (1994) *Describing Language*. 2nd ed. Buckingham: Open University Press.

Hendrick, S. (2004) *Understanding Close Relationships*. Boston: Pearson.

Hodgman, L. (2011) *Enabling Environments in the Early Years*. London: Practical Pre-School Books.

Jingbo, L. & Elicker, J. (2005) 'Teacher-Child Interaction in Chinese Kindergartens: An Observational Analysis.' *International Journal of Early Years Education* 13(2): 129–143. http://dx.doi.org/10.1080/09669760500171139 (accessed 23 July 2013).

McSporran, E. (1997) 'Towards Better Listening and Learning in the Classroom.' *Educational Review* 49 (1): 13–20.

Miller, L. & Cable, C. (2012) *Professionalism in the Early Years*. London: Hodder Education.

Mitchell, P. & Ziegler, F. (2007) *Fundamentals of Development: The Psychology of Childhood*. Hover: Psychology Press/Taylor & Francis.

Moss, P. & Petrie, P. (2002) *From Children's Services to Children's Spaces*. New York: Routledge Falmer.

Moyles, J. (Ed) (2010) *The Excellence of Play*. New York: Open University Press.

NMoER (2006) *Framework Plan for the Content and Tasks of Kindergarten*. Oslo: Norwegian Ministry of Education and Research.

NMoER (2012) *Framework Plan for the Content and Tasks of Kindergarten*. www.regjeringen. no/upload/KD/Vedlegg/Barnehager/engelsk/Framework_Plan_for_the_content_and_Tasks_ of_Kindergartens_2011.pdf (accessed 14 January 2014).

Norwegian Ministry of Children & Equality (2008) *The Rights of the Child*. www.regjeringen.no/ upload/BLD/Barnets%20rettigheter/The_Rights_of_the_Child.pdf#search=Kindergarten% 20framework%20plan%20%202006%20in%20English (accessed 3 August 2013).

Nutbrown, C. (2013) *Foundations for Quality*. www.education.gov.uk/nutbrownreview (accessed 24 July 2013).

Nutkins, S., McDonald, C. & Stephen, M. (2013) *Early Childhood Education and Care: An Introduction*. London: SAGE.

Oates, R. & Sanders, A. (2009) 'Making a Little Difference for Early Childhood Studies Students.' In T. Papatheodoru & J. Moyles (eds), *Learning Together in the Early Years: Exploring Relational Pedagogy*. London: Routledge.

OHCHR (2009) 'Committee on the Rights of the Child to Be Heard – General Comments.' www2.ohchr.org/english/bodies/crc/comments.htm (accessed 23 July 2013).

Oswell, D. (2012) *The Agency of Children: From Family to Global Human Rights*. Cambridge: Cambridge University Press.

Page, J., Clare, A. & Nutbrown, C. (2013) *Working with Babies & Children from Birth to Three*. London: SAGE.

Palaiologou, I. (Ed) (2013) *The Early Years Foundation Stage*. London: SAGE.

Penn, H. (2011) *Quality in Early Childhood Services: An International Perspective*. Berks: McGraw Hill.

Petrie, P. (2011) *Communicating Skills for Working with Children and Young People: Introducing Social Pedagogy*. London: Jessica Kingsley.

Riley, J. (Ed) (2007) *Learning in the Early Years*. London: SAGE.

Rinaldi, C. (2005) *In Dialogue with Reggio Emilia*. London: RoutledgeFalmer.

Rogers, C.R. (1961) *On Becoming a Person: A Therapist's View of Psychotherapy*. London: Constable.

Rose, J. & Rogers S. (2012) *The Role of the Adult in Early Years Settings*. Berks: Open University Press.

Roulstone, S., Law, J., Rush, R., Clegg, J. & Peters, T. (2011) 'Investigating the Role of Language in Children's Early Educational Outcomes.' *Research Report DFE-RR134*. www.gov.uk/government/uploads/system/uploads/attachment_data/file/181549/DFE-RR134 (accessed 30 July 2013).

Smidt, S. (2009) *Introducing Vygotsky: A Guide for Practitioners and Students in Early Years Education*. London: Routledge.

Smidt, S. (2011) *Introducing Bruner: A Guide for Practitioners and Students in Early Years Education*. London: Routledge.

Smith, P.K., Cowie, H. & Blades, M. (2011) *Understanding Children's Development*. Chichester: Wiley.

Tholin, K.R. & Jansen, T.T. (2012) 'Something to Talk About: Does the Language Use of Pre-school Teachers Invite Children to Participate in Democratic Conversation?' *European Early Childhood Education Research Journal* 20(1): 35–46. http://dx.doi/10.1080/13502 93X.2012.650010 (accessed 23 July 2013).

Trevarthen, C. (2005) 'First Things First: Infants Make Good Use of Sympathetic Rhythm, of Imitation, without Reason or Language.' *Journal of Child Psychotherapy* 31 (1): 91–113.

UNCRC (1989) United Nations Convention on the Rights of the Child. UNICEF. Available at: http://www.unicef.org.uk/Document-pdfs/UNCRC_PRESS200910web.pdf (Accessed February 2014)

Winnicott, D. (1971) *Play and Reality*. London: Routledge.

Winter, K. (2011) *Building Relationships and Communicating with Young Children: A Practical Guide for Social Workers*. London: Routledge.

Chapter 6

The critically reflective practitioner

Andrew Sanders

By the end of this chapter you will:

- Have explored what critically reflective practice is and, more importantly, what it might mean for you.
- Have considered some strategies to bring this kind of professional development from theory into reality.
- Have started to think about becoming engaged in some personal and collaborative learning processes which may offer models for and evidence of continuing personal and work-based growth.

Some first thoughts

A past civil engineer friend once said:

> . . . if a building stays up then it's good architecture; if it falls down, then it's bad engineering.

This may capture one key feature of critically reflective practice, in that it is probably more about aesthetics, intent, design and an occupied space than it might be about the nuts-and-bolts physics of construction. However, it may well be that the detail of construction *is* also required to assure a beautiful and durable result – a combination, therefore, of architecture *and* engineering.

In a historical sense, Jeremy Bentham (cited in Lively & Lively 1994) also suggested that we should spend some time considering not only looking back at some of the technical detail of what we might do but also the overall ambience, possible effect (utility) and flavour of what we might be doing, in our case when working with children and their families – what he might have called an 'architecture of reflection'.

This chapter addresses this challenge, as noted in the Reflecting Girl (Figure 6.1).

The following comes in two unequal parts; first, we have some rationale as to the shape and style of the content of the chapter and, by implication, second, some consequent thoughts about how to begin to 'do' critical reflection itself.

Figure 6.1 Reflecting Girl

The reflecting practitioner:

Think about yourself, your actions, your reflections on your actions and then what it felt like to reflect! (meta-reflection)

Introduction

This part of the book addresses some issues that I believe to be important for participants through their journey. It builds upon previous chapters. Along the way, the text is peppered with diagrams and information boxes; these are designed to offer some points of enlightenment for the reader.

Crucially, the value of reflection as one facet of professional development is recognised; it is important to 'encourage reflection and refinement' (Nutbrown 2012:56). It is perhaps the 'refinement' which may suggest moving forward in a more advanced manner – probably towards a more critical stance.

Moving forward, there are now some further final underpinning pieces of the jigsaw that are considered to be crucial; the contribution of the critical element of reflective practice. These can be taken forward as 'transferable approaches', key skills applied on the lifelong journey. It is also important in this chapter not to expect a series of solutions and answers as the author considers pointers and nudges to be more appropriate to critically reflective practice.

This text divides into three parts: Part One explores features, Part Two considers realization and Part Three offers examples.

Part one: features, barriers and context

Doing it or not?

Being critically reflective may offer a goal, but it is not guaranteed; before we get into the meat of the subject, there are possibly some dangers in *not* adopting a (critically) reflective approach. Leeson usefully points out (cited in Parker-Rees *et al.* 2010:180) that

> unless we engage in this process, the work we do has the potential to be ill-informed and possibly dangerous as we perpetuate actions and decisions that no longer have relevance, simply because that is the way it has always been done and no one questions it.

Thompson and Thompson (2008:8) help us in this area as well. As students you all have active and full lives, but 'the busier we are, the more reflective we need to be'. In addition, they point out that it is something that needs to be consciously worked at; it is enhanced if shared and a vital component in professional development which synthesises theory and doing.

Sometimes reflection can get stuck; it becomes an exercise focused on whether the activity itself was successful, and whether the children enjoyed it (Bryant cited in Evans 2011b).

On a more positive side, however, reflection is arguably a fundamental part of 'self' and the kind of recall as a starting point clearly involves the use of memory. We are warned that 'without personal memory, we are unable to satisfactorily construct a viable sense of self' (Abrams 2010:82). Moving further, if our individual identities are at least partly culturally constructed (see box), then we might see that each of us needs to undergo a process of telling ourselves (and others) a story about ourselves. These stories (Linde cited in Abrams 2010) may contain three features:

- A sense of past, present (and future); temporal continuity.
- A sense of self apart from others.
- Perhaps connected more with an oral history tradition, a reflexive element not dissimilar to an ongoing (re)interpretative process within the conversation; a recounting in the light of the 'present self'.

The final one is usefully elaborated upon as a 'distinction between the narrator (the person doing the telling) and the protagonist (the person at the centre of the story) of the narrative' (Linde cited in Abrams 2010:39).

This 'distinction' has a feeling of stepping outside oneself, and we will be visiting this again later; it certainly does have a cerebral tone, though, and suggests maybe a kind of personal epiphany and a life-changing experience.

We seem to see the dangers of irrelevance and superficiality, and it appears that it may be the result of a deliberate and conscious effort and be a necessary part of us.

Implementation, features and context

Reflective practice, therefore, is presented here as a *very simple process*, and in some ways, the core notion is that real-life application (and reflection upon this) is at least as important as the theories which underpin it. In short, the *process of doing it* is probably the central objective. After all, this is not seen to be a sterile academic exercise but a real opportunity to think about what scaffolds our (reflective) thinking.

In contrast to a technical manual or set of instructions, considering reflective practice as a design and 'aesthetic' might move us forward – an architecture with impact, a shape and structure that may enable us to move towards making a difference in the real lives of children and their families through professional work based on genuine critically reflective practice.

There are some interim features of this perspective; some of these may include some of the following points:

A first priority might be that, having learned earlier about some of the skills needed to be reflective practitioners, students now need to move forward and apply it, *buy into it* and demonstrate that they can evidence it. And really do it. This means that the platform for reflection must be clearly and comfortably established; practitioners need to have belief and commitment. The primary purpose here is to support the *real application of reflection* – critical reflection, in particular.

Embedded reflective practitioner skills that sit as a foundation approach which inform the building of a positive relationship-based pedagogical position with children. In other words, a key factor which can influence what goes on in the co-constructed meaning-making zone between adult and child is underpinned by a *being-with* stance (Petrie *et al.* 2006).

Without trivialising core aspects of reflective activities, the writer considers, for the purposes of everyday practice (which might be, for children, what really matters), students, of course, need first to accept, understand and try out processes and be supported by skilful tutors and mentors. There is also evidence to indicate that reflection can benefit from knowledgeable and informed preparation and intervention (Schofield 2009). It becomes something that can be framed and supported by perhaps more experienced process-oriented mentors and tutors; more than just reviewing content?

Next, and more importantly, evidence suggests that they may require, then, a framework (Moon 2003, 2008) and space (real and/or virtual) to critically share and explore their experiences, both as descriptive narratives and reflective (analytical) feelings.

This may have three dimensions – first, what actually went on? And then, second, what do I think about what happened? And finally, what was the process like and where can I take it to enhance my practice? Importantly, we note here that these statements all end with a question mark. All are irrefutably linked, of course. It is also argued that this is a challenging process especially when attempted to do by oneself – a bit like having a conversation with oneself. To turn this internal conversation into a dialogue with others helps and may add richness to the experience of the process. To engage, contribute and be a member of a learning community-of-practice which shares a conversation is therefore a rewarding opportunity and experience together. Add to this an objective of promoting an enduring and trusted collaborative learning and teaching environment.

This is not easy, and the 'architecture' may need support and some 'scaffolding'. The overall aim is to consciously focus on the creation and realization of elementary disciplines associated with being critically reflective, perhaps facilitating a personal reflective space, sometimes shared, sometimes personal, occasionally virtual where this process can take place.

Barriers?

As mentioned before, there are obviously some challenges (barriers) here, and Eaton (cited in Evans 2011a:24) points out that, in essence, 'people find reflection quite difficult'. Some of these obstacles might include the following.

Some participants, typically, are time-poor – invariably, and sometimes by necessity, combining earning and learning. This means that opportunities for, say, collaborative learning and real and meaningful exchange are limited. Strategies to make the best of what we have, 'expand' this time and opportunity and to add flexibility to these are important.

Some people often have some experience, some a store of years of working with very young children in many different capacities and roles. Other (often younger) students have had less opportunity to build up a repertoire of encounters. This means that *how* reflection takes place and what it means can be very different (Fook & Askeland 2007). Indeed importantly, it needs to be relevant to the individual.

Some belief in sharing next. Experience with students (another, as yet, unpublished activity) suggests that some participants do not believe that they alone have an authoritative and valid set of experiences; least of all, it seems, do they wish to publicise their 'inadequacies'. A hierarchical view of what is acceptable and legitimate knowledge seems to be very strong. (This is possibly to do with the prevailing university image and construct, or previous ways of learning and their associated messages.) Ways of working here therefore need to clearly articulate this dilemma and address it, at least, subliminally but also sometimes upfront.

> There are some different views about this in the private sector, though (Berthelemy 2009). The taking part in collaborative activity can be regarded as being a real and positive attribute which is rewarded – a sort-of competition to be non-competitive but still underpinned by the financial reward ethic.

The feeling of competition is also important. Towards the end of the first decade of the new century, neo-liberal approaches may inform a discourse within the UK early years landscape. When considering essential collaborative activities, some participants are understandably steeped in some of the values of the UK education system; these might include an individualistic emphasis and a micromanaged work ethos with a performance and monitoring mindset. This makes sharing and collaborative learning quite difficult – an affront to everything that has gone before; sharing may be perceived as 'giving away advantage'.

At this stage following consideration of our commitment and implementation, we do not, of course, wish to dwell on the barriers. But it might be useful to explore what a critically reflective practitioner might be.

Part two: realization, analysis and 'theory'

Practitioner

Yates with Appleby in Chapter Three allude to this as well, but we all, it appears, believe the term 'practitioner' to be problematic with an overly mechanistic and technical feel (Moss 2008). For those who are dispensing education from a book (of targets, competencies and guidance) this may be appropriate, but this doesn't do any favours to the professionalism and autonomy, skills, insights and confidences that adults draw upon to offer the best support for children and young people in the process of 'growing up' (Browne 2008). In the UK, the framework for children's care and education is (as the time of writing) bounded by the Early Years Foundation Stage (DCSF 2008a) and reinforced by punitive and persuasive regulatory levers. The word used is 'practitioner', and for ease of understanding in this chapter, I shall use this word interchangeably with the word 'educator'.[1]

By way of further consideration, though, practitioners are expected to be researchers, and there may well be a certain relationship here with engagement in the process of personal development. This introspective and investigative 'research' stance can sometimes feel a little lofty – aligned possibly with connotations around the word 'research'. Toning down the title might help. Words like 'enquirer' and 'explorer' come to mind (Fisher 2008).

We will revisit 'research' a little later, but there is little doubt that whatever people who work with children and their families might be called, there is a notion of action, doing and change.

Criticality

One main theme of this chapter is to consider what it might *mean* to *be* a critically reflective practitioner. We've already had a look at the last word in this phrase, which leaves us with the 'critically' and the 'reflective' bits.

It is difficult to be prescriptive here – thus this section will explore a range of dilemmas, positions and approaches; readers can thus move forward in the way they may wish to. Turning first, then, to the 'critically' bit. This, for many, may have a negative feel to it – a nagging, chipping-away, downbeat, hangdog approach on the mild side as against an aggressive, argumentative, challenging, confrontational and threatening sense at another, more extreme end. Of course, it can be (m)any of these and can change over time.

What we want to do here is to gradually move towards a personal (personal to you, not to me) deconstruction of critical theory and pedagogy. The stance therefore is not a prescriptive one, the aim being to present a basic framework or architectural 'room' (space) within which individuals may shape and furnish the interior to their individual taste, desire and pocket.

This *does* involve some serious reflection and dialogue, though.

Figure 6.2 The full stop and the comma

This has been talked about in previous chapters – for example, in Chapter Two's discussion of the role of the student as researcher – an educator developing insight through organized and thoughtful enquiry. I believe there to be another, alternative way of looking at (traditional) 'research', one which has as much to do with the researcher him- or herself as it does with his or her subject. We can call this critical research, and this is, in turn, closely associated with our role as 'critically reflective practitioners'.

Critical research, firstly, therefore,

> must be connected to an attempt to confront the injustice of a particular society or public sphere within a society. [It] . . . becomes a transformative endeavour unembarrassed by the label 'political' and unafraid to consummate a relationship with emancipatory consciousness.
>
> (Kincheloe & McLaren 2005:305)

Not only, then, do researchers publicly position themselves in this role but also embrace and own their (research) actions, often organic (grounded theory), as the first step in what can essentially be described as a *political* process – that is, to do with Foucauldian power and change. The educator, therefore, is an actor, a participant in change through, in our case, an education process – in short, one who is exercising a critical pedagogy. One may also consider provisionality, Figure 6.2 simplifies.

The full stop and the comma . . . think of a sentence (any sentence) and new discourses. Modernism is represented by a full stop; it's an end, the finish, a sentence that's completed. The comma suggests that there's more to come, a next thought, something coming after (post-); knowledge as provisional, on the way, always becoming.

Individual or social?

An important point needs to be made here: one style of critically reflective practice (learning and getting better from looking at the past as a personal journey) may be at one end of the reflective scale. This would represent, perhaps, a more 'individual and isolationist' (Morrison 1996:318) position. In contrast, towards the opposite end, might be more one which addresses a *critical* political or social dimension. Here the critically reflective approach might be asking 'postmodern' questions. To move towards the latter does take more directed time and thought. An action dimension and a strong

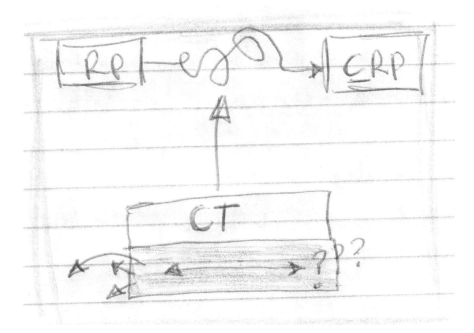

Figure 6.3 Journey from reflective practice to critically reflective practice

relationship between pedagogy and society may be one element that sets the second style apart from perhaps more traditional and arguably less demanding models – a conscious awareness of presence, effect and process (see Linde cited in Abrams 2010). It is the development of the second which forms the guiding principle of this chapter, though they are not mutually exclusive. Indeed, it may be that the first is a prerequisite on the way to the second. Moving on, we consider Figure 6.3 where, in short, we move from reflective practice to critically reflective practice through the application of *our* critical theory. We need to own it; it is probably what we choose it to be, where we might be on the critical agenda.

Second, what *is* critical theory? What kind of critical theory applies? Where does it come in to make a critical pedagogy?

There are different degrees of critical theory; they range from those linked to grand narratives (see Habermas 1976) towards Derridian deconstructed relativism (see Royle 2003). We need to explore where we might be on this scale. And there probably isn't a way round this apart from judicious, selective and dedicated reading on the subject.

One of the challenges of critical theory is that it shows itself in many ways and is always changing. Most difficult is that it's probably quite woolly, and this makes it subject to disagreement. Generally, though, in a sense, it is *contraire* – against old ways of interpreting the world.

It may involve a central notion of challenge linked with reflective practice and to the 'post-' discourses, though. In order to question things, though, we probably need some sort of platform, a base. A couple of short points, then.

Figure 6.4 Happiness

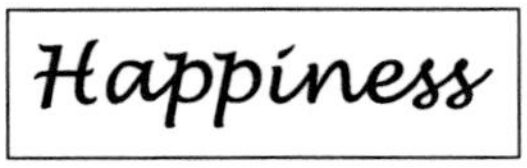

Figure 6.5 Happiness

Firstly, if we recall the full stop and the comma and apply this to, say, a theory of knowledge, then we don't have any hard-and-fast states of post-ism, just an understanding that it rejects, and is critical of, what interpretations about what knowledges might have been dominant in the past. Critical theory embraces provisionality and uncertainty (Urban 2008; Moss 2010).

Secondly, in order to reflect on our practice (for example), we may need to have a body of knowledge against which to apply it. Is it a kind of understanding that we are aware of and is replicable, explicit and informed? Or is it implicit, a 'gut response' derived from an unknown source? (Thompson & Thompson 2008). We need to explore where we might be coming from, so to speak.

Thirdly, we may need to make visible the previously hidden. Harvey Danger sings that 'Happiness writes white' – in other words, we need to recognise something that we take for granted and to make it 'appear' requires a change of background. Please see Figures 6.4 and 6.5 for clarity.

A desired start, then, is that we have an obviously open approach, but this needs to be paralleled with a *direction* to channel our energies. If we're going to challenge, we need a subject and a strategy. Among others, for example, Bronfenbrenner's ecological model (1994) could help us with this in that the landscape is divided up, aligning concentric circles around the child – much more on this later.

Referring to 'happiness' previously, we may need to explore the colour of the script or the tone of the background to render things visible. Connected with this, Mac Naughton (2006:6) reminds us that 'reflective educators need to be inquisitive and sceptical' before we can move forward. But we can't do this just by ourselves; it involves connection with the people who create and are influenced by the microcosm.

Returning to looking at the individual and the social, we need to explore, for example, why things are how they are. This is a dialogic process – that is, it's about who we are and who others might be. The first basic practice, then, is to lay bare, challenge and change a person's *individual* understandings and actions.

'Individual' is an important word. When we prefix the words 'reflective practice' with 'critical', we move beyond the personal realm towards

> the operation and effects of the power relationships *between* people . . . seeking to analyse oppressive and inequitable power relationships with students [and children] and then use *their* analysis to work against that oppression and inequity. (Mac Naughton 2006:7)

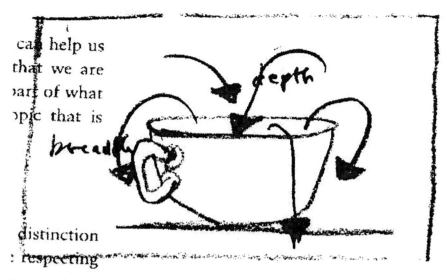

Figure 6.6 Coffee cup

This may relate to the implicit/explicit consideration mentioned above.

It is both individual and social at the same time. So, as a second basic practice, what has slipped in here is another dimension. We have thinking about individuals in the context of their wider social surroundings – as part of 'the bigger picture'. We need to consider some of the more overarching things that might be going on (e.g. oppression and inequity) which affect our ways of doing and thinking. Looking at these as contextual background – although guardedly sometimes – often we can do very little about these on a big scale, but they may mediate in little ways when working with young children.

So critical thinking has these two dimensions – individual and social – and when directed at our own (and others') practice, it moves towards critically reflective practice. This could be pictured where the subject might be, say, a coffee cup (see Figure 6.6) where the lines of enquiry could be described at individual (depth) and social (breadth).

The coffee cup:

we need to look inside the cup – what's the strength, has it got milk? – as well as outside it – who boiled the water and why? Is it a mug or bone china cup and saucer? Where was it fired? What kind of table is it on, round, a desk . . . and where is the table and why?

Underpinning these 'anti' and dialogical approaches, arguably, are the sociological approaches and theories promoted by the Frankfurt School in the second half of the twentieth century, led by Jürgen Habermas. Even earlier, this approach is probably founded in Socratic dialogue and what Foucault (cited in Gros 2010) more contemporarily names as 'parrēsia' (meaning [a spirit of] 'free-spokeness').

> Quirkily, Michel Foucault is recorded to have said, 'My job is making windows where there once were walls' (Hyde cited in White 2007:26). This is useful in that it reflects criticality as an approach, rather than a solution.

Further, in a brief review by Mac Naughton (2008), critical approaches, in early years at least, may centre on 'possibilities for a better world'. There is also a 'change mentality' linked to exploring sceptically the big principles and ideas that inform and applying these directly to what really happens – that is, practice.

So, in summary then, following an individual analysis of ourselves and our position, we point towards a challenging, crucial 'look behind' what's going on and articulation of the ideologies and power structures which may inform current practice under scrutiny. Putting such concepts 'on the table' enables their critical exploration.

This is not easy.

Challenges

Here we explore asking questions, 'wobbling' and visualising.

One problem is that often dominant discourses and ideology are so powerful and all-embracing that we take them for granted – they're disguised. All this 'theory' is okay but we may need an example: let's take 'carpet time', for example.

We know that children all come to our setting with a different history of experiences (Bourdieu cited in Haralambos & Holborn 2004); we see, for example, that not all youngsters can sit down and listen during carpet time. Quietly attending to a group story here is an expectation, but why? Is it for efficiency? Is it to do with order and organization, strategies that promote the good of the many over the few? Does this promote better learning for all, in a settled, balanced and organized way?

'Yes' is probably the answer to all of these – but why? Why can't children get stuck into books that interest them by themselves? Why is listening apparently so hard? Which children have the experience and wherewithal to take part and why? Who might this leave out, why might it exclude and should it? What do we do about it?

A second challenge is that we might just be reminded, in these times, not to delve too deeply into what seems to be small, mainstream, familiar and seemingly insignificant points, but we do need to be 'inquisitive and sceptical' (as mentioned earlier). We may need to assert that 'apparently familiar things need first to be made strange' (Bauman 2010:4); to unsettle (or 'wobble') a situation.

We're beginning here to explore some of the ideologies that may surround, in this example, a group storytelling activity, but, more importantly, we're looking at the set of circumstances that have come to describe what might be appropriate behaviour. We are starting to look at the mechanisms that reinforce this or that way of doing things – beginning to address the 'false consciousness', the mask or façade that persuades us that there's no other way.

Furthermore, Habermas, aligned with Foucault (cited in Dalton 2008), notes that we can be free only when we can choose our truths. And we can do this only when our position is truly critically reflected upon and we can *see* the power structures that we think exist, the tools which assure its continued domination. Even further, strategies emerge which might point to being liberated from the mix (turning theory into practice . . . what Freire [1975] refers to as 'praxis'). There are elements here of not only the process of critical reflection but also the purpose and outcome of practicing it. For Habermas (1976), this objective might include possibilities for a more fair society, democracy, empowerment and emancipation.

Clearly there are big levers at play here; this is a journey and certainly not an overnight one, one probably and realistically working generally towards an 'evolving criticality . . . and [being] an awkward detective' (Kincheloe & McClaren 2005:306).[2]

Moving forward, critical pedagogy therefore is an educational stance which has as one of its goals the emancipation of social connections . . . perhaps towards a more just world, depending on your critical position or where you might sit on the scale. The really important point is that the *process* of critical reflection is the turning point, aligned with the overall objective (whatever this may be).

Stepping back, there's always a temptation to attempt to replace a standard belief with another set of certainties, if only to retain one's sanity! It's all well and good to say that we, as critically reflective actors, need to move into this complex arena, but it's no breeze; this practice begins to challenge and places us as agents of change on the cusp of innovation. Indeed, the very inquisitiveness and scepticism mentioned earlier essentially combined with action dimensions serves to ask questions.

Perhaps, on a more fundamental level, we need to accept, and be comfortable with, other ways of exploring discourse and creating new knowledge and simply celebrate its contribution. And that the answer may well be evasive, personal and ultimately indeterminate. Returning to the comma and full stop, really. . . .

So, after having looked at the context of our coffee cup, some 'breadth and depth enquiry' and wobbling, we will now look at the reflection element; we want here to apply our revitalised stance to the way we learn from the past and ultimately improve (our) practice.

Somewhat related, it's useful to have a look at what Mead (cited in Smith & Nicolson 2011) says about the relationship between the content of life history and the present/future. Continuing the post-stance of Osgood (2010) (unsettling), we see that Mead puts forward the idea that when we recall, we see the life journey as marked by schisms and our responses to them at the time. Reflection then is selective but it has lessons for us. Consider, for example, that:

> . . . the past is part of the experienced living present . . . a social response to disruptions in the past that continue to influence the present. Individuals . . . live 'in the present' but also 'out of the past'. (Smith & Nicolson 2011:38)

The past and present are thus linked and they may together foreshadow the future. The historical 'I', the contemporary and reflexive 'me' and the future 'to be', if you like.

Reflection

Thinking back about a situation could be what reflection is about, but it's probably a bit more complicated than that. Sometimes it occurs when we're unsure about something that's happened or if something we encounter surprises or 'wobbles' us. And we *do* need to account for it and evidence this.

At its core is the opportunity that reflection gives us to develop our professionalism through emerging strategies for (self) improvement. It can also perhaps help us to more fully understand and appreciate our identity.

Many people have said many things about reflection; some questions you may have could include: Can all professionals reflect? Are the ones who do it better at their jobs? It can be to do with context (the surrounding conditions) or in response to an unexpected incident; often it's not an end in itself but poses more questions about new issues. Reframing (adjusting our belief set to accommodate new experiences) seems to be a constant theme, and Farrelly (2010:26) usefully points out that

> it has been generally agreed that through this process new understandings and appreciations may be acquired and problems reframed. Many authors write about three stages of reflection: first, the awareness of uncomfortable feelings or thoughts; second, critical analysis of those feelings; and third, the uncovering of new perspectives.

When we add this reframing to our objective of discourse disclosure and (uncertain) relativity, then we have a definite challenge. It may well be wise to be very selective in our choice of subject. For instance, to account for the entire workings of a day-in-nursery may create (for ourselves) an unachievable task – much better then to observe just an incident which suggests uneasiness ('wobbles' us). Not only might this selective strategy limit the enquiry but offer us realistic hope.

As explained earlier, knowing about the benefits of reflection is one thing; actually putting it into practice is quite another. Perhaps this isn't surprising in the light of the tasks outlined earlier.

Why reflect critically?

It is argued here that as a participant engaged in an occupation which involves people (in our case, children, who could be seen as a vulnerable group), we need more than just academic competence. We also need, in our context as early years practitioners and educators, confidence, skills, insight and sensitivity, to name a few, to judge when intervention may be appropriate – to do this we need, often minute-by-minute, to balance our professionalism with our value base and ethics of care.

In parallel, this will have a lot to do with our past experiences, employing these positively. We do, therefore

> need to develop our self-awareness and capacity for critical reflection in order to ensure that our motivation and past experiences are used to enhance our practice.
> (Lishman cited in Adams 2009:375)

Looking at *reflection*, then, our first element is that it's not just about the now – it's also about where we are now and how we got there. Secondly, it's about ourselves, our development, where we are now and where we might go (on the reflective journey) and our ambitions . . .

Using an example, in the UK, much is trumpeted about 'quality', another essentially socially constructed notion. It is *generally* accepted that quality provision probably includes thinking and progressive educators.

Our third element about reflection is that there are some features, however, which need emphasising:

> Beauty is in the eye of the beholder. In other words, reflective practice is a personal position; it is, for individuals, a way-of-seeing. In essence, then, a creative activity based on personal interpretation and context understanding. What, I think, it is not is a scientific process, nor mechanistic, nor 'worker-as-technician'.
>
> (Moss 2008:xiii)

So, this is about the content and context of our coffee cup; maybe a few outline starting definitions of reflection might also be handy here, pointing us towards

> an active process whereby the professional can gain an understanding of how historical, social, cultural, cognitive and personal experiences have contributed to personal knowledge acquisition and practice. An examination of such factors yields an opportunity to identify new potentials within practice, thus challenging the constraints of habituated thoughts and practices. The process of reflective practice can be guided by the use of a form of supervision. Through the exploration of individual and social behaviour and experiences, there is scope to gain insights to challenge and guide professional practice.
>
> (Wilkinson 1996:36)

and

> a rigorous process of meaning-making, a continuous process of constructing theories of the world, testing them through dialogue and listening, then reconstructing those theories.
>
> (Moss 2008:xiii)

In addition,

> Critical reflection is dialogic. It requires social connections with others; conversations with others; support from others, colleagues willing to spend time with you and a chance to share ideas and possibilities with others.
>
> (Mac Naughton 2008:5)

The critically reflective journey, then, is personal and social, active and rigorous. Additionally, this might suggest that:

- It's something that we do (about ourselves), sometimes with others.
- It requires a 'pedagogy of listening' (Rinaldi 2005); a connection.
- Something we have to work at (Moon 2008).
- Something we have to believe in for it to work well and that requires 'space'.

- We may need a model . . . any model. Perhaps a step-by-step suggestion could include: description, information, confrontation and reconstruction (Smythe 1989).
- Informs lifelong learning and considered 'position'.

Things to do and think about, on your own or together

- Find out what others say about the circular nature of reflective practice and what might be the differences.
- Based on Tindal (2006), you could try to note an experience where you are consciously reflecting *in* action. Then apply (retrospective) reflection *on* action to the same event. This exercise may enable a comparison and help to analyse the value of Schön's thoughts.

Furthermore, one important feature remains – that any 'theory' offers, at least, a purpose and framework; arguably this is probably not a path to tread alone, and sensitive support is required along the way.

Becoming (and being) a critically reflective practitioner is as an insightful doer, communicator and facilitator and has something to do with applying a radical, sceptical exploratory and broad stance informed by critical process. We revisit here the reflective practitioner.

So, some of the elements of what it might mean to be a critically reflective practitioner have been briefly explored; taking our action perspective, crucially now we need to look at some aspects which may illustrate some further challenges, ways of doing it, others' experiences and the like.

Part three: some examples and strategies

Models of reflective practice

When we examine some models of reflective practice (Gibbs 1988; Kolb 1984; Mezirow *et al.* 1990), they mostly seem to offer a pictorially 'round' process; the spiral bit comes in (in a 3D sense) to offer another dimension – not just left and

Figure 6.7 Donald Schön

right but up and down. Put simply, a Plan, Do, Review model . . . and then apply it next time, to get better; ascend, go up.

Donald Schön offers a sound starting point, and other authors in this volume have written about the value of his core tool of reflecting-*in*-action and reflection-*on*-action, but, like Convery (1998), I suspect that it's probably not enough. Structures that support the more critical and action/change-oriented processes deriving from the basic platform may well be required . . . and these, in turn, require a definite and distinct space to allow this expansionary activity to occur. There might be something here about the conditions required for critical practice to thrive.

Donald Schön (1930–1997) was a bigger thinker than just the work on reflective practice, but it was this aspect particularly that seems to have stood the test of time. He did his doctorate on Dewey's work and was influenced by Dewey's thoughts about 'inquiry learning'. And that it's almost a style of living that accepts that we're all encountering new situations every day and we somehow (maybe to retain our sanity, if anything?) need to accommodate these dimensions of change into our personal constructs. So learning is a discover-account-for-and-readjust process that goes on all the time. Schön was also a very good jazz and light classical musician.

Some further strategies

Colleagues will have addressed useful frameworks to make reflection worthwhile and practical; the overall list is extensive but here are some others that might help. This is not, we recall, an engineering manual, nor a set of instructions.

Morrison (1996:320) also helps us further with some feasible stages by citing Habermas (1976:230):

- Stage One: a description and interpretation of the existing situation – a hermeneutic exercise that identifies and attempts to make sense of the current curricular and pedagogical practices which obtain in a situation.
- Stage Two: a penetration of the reasons that brought the existing situation to the form that it takes – the causes and purposes of a situation and an evaluation of their legitimacy, involving an analysis of interests at work in a situation, their power and legitimacy. For Habermas a full analysis requires attention to micro and macro forces which operate in a situation.
- Stage Three: an agenda for altering the situation – in order for moves to an egalitarian society to be furthered.
- Stage Four: an evaluation of the achievement of the agenda in practice.

To continue the architecture analogy, above all, we need to feel comfortable with the feel of the space and be pleased with its design and function before we can look at some of the possible personally selected furniture, fixtures and fittings.

There's many ways of doing it around (see earlier boxes), and I would just want to put forward some others – namely, the 'practitioner map': 'What, So What, Now What' (Driscoll 2000; Gibbs 1988).

In practitioner maps, as explored by Clark (2010), this applies to the 'mosaic' approach but this time applied not just with children but also with childcare educators. Based on setting research, a broader approach is beginning to be developed, one which considers

> Documentation produced by young children and adults [which together creates] the opportunity for different perspectives to be considered in designing and reviewing early childhood spaces.
>
> (Clark 2010:52)

Simplicity is often the key. Given the practical issues of time and space, insights often occur inconveniently. This means that if you're on a bus or waiting for root canal work at the dentist when groundbreaking thoughts happen, then they can be noted. A way of recording is required and this can be almost anything: a smartphone, slips of paper, a diary.

Have a look at Table 6.1, referring to 'What? So What? Now What?' (Driscoll 2000), Farrelly (2010:29) notes that

> this offers quite a succinct way of recording events and the headings are so broad you could really write (note/record) as much as you like.

You can see the highlighted letters in Account, Interpret and Extrapolate (AIE). You could use AIE as headings in a notebook. The important point is to *do it*. You can, having done this, revisit it (reflectively) later, like documentation. The process of doing it and what it felt like (see Figure 6.1) can also be added and reviewed later.

Gibbs's circular descriptive models are shown in Figures 6.8 and 6.9.

Along similar lines, it might be that some people like more of a framework, especially one which might accommodate the bits and pieces of feelings and emotions.

Table 6.1 What? So What? Now What?

What?	Take the event and just describe it (**a**ccount).
So What?	Think about what it means to you, and analyse why it might mean this to you (**i**nterpret).
Now What?	Explain how you might apply this new learning when you come across this in the future (**e**xtrapolate).

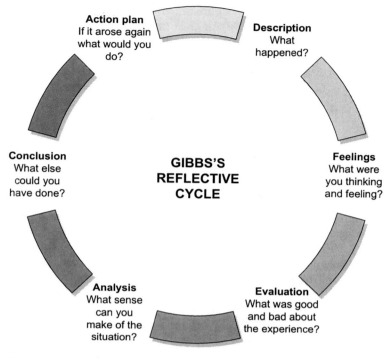

Figure 6.8 Gibbs (1, 1998)

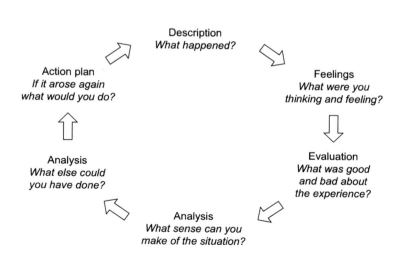

Figure 6.9 Gibbs (2, 1998)

These (feelings) are clearly important but sometimes subsumed or thought to be not what is required (in your studies). Buying in, I think, is not entirely rational so these need to be there. Gibbs (1988) might help us here.

Looking at Gibbs's diagram, you can see perhaps the more 'thoughtful' sections in Feelings and Analysis and a reference to your (inevitable) values in Evaluation. Practically, this might be an improvement for you; importantly, it depends on you.

Summary

Commentators and course participants often note that this discussion has opened up the field of (design) possibilities rather than offered some hard and fast engineering certainties. Students coming to critically reflective practice and ideas that surround it tend to look for certainties and are disappointed – indeed, one could say, the last thing that's needed in the final year of the degree! But it might well be just that – an approach that has the potential to take us forward.

At the start of this chapter, we notioned that critically reflective practice could be architecture or engineering. Uncertainty probably means some level of interpretive effort; the challenge here is not and has not set out to be anything akin to inform, educate or advise but to point to and promote an environment in which the participant has the opportunity to go towards what might make meaning for him or her – engaging possibilities for insightful, sensitive and empathetic practice with effective *real* professional development. Not pure engineering then – probably both.

This chapter has outlined and addressed some key points which may support using some of the approaches related to critically reflective practice. Some potential barriers have been made visible. More importantly, it may have offered some real and manageable initial, and unashamedly personal, strategies which could result in putting some critically reflective approaches into practice.

A short review of our first learning aims indicates some qualified success, qualified because the process *is* a journey and it *is* an individual one. The rationale behind the extensive, but certainly not exhaustive, reference list ahead is for just this reason. And it *is* a reference list; it may just offer possible starting points for further investigation towards both personal and professional development on that critical voyage of discovery.

Notes

1. Looking at later information in *More Great Childcare* (DfE 2013), the word 'practitioner' seems to have been superseded by 'teacher' and 'educator'.
2. Peter Falk's character in the US detective programme, 'Columbo', used this to good effect.

References and further reading

Abrams, L. (2010) *Oral History Theory*. Abingdon: Routledge.
Adams, R., Dominelli, L. & Payne, M. (2009) *Social Work: Themes, Issues and Perspectives*. Basingstoke: MacMillan.
Bauman, Z. (2010) *44 Letters from the Liquid Modern World*. Cambridge: Polity.

Berthelemy, M. (2009, 18 November) *A Conversation with Mark*. University of Derby. Personal discussion between the author and Mark Berthelemy.

Bertram, T. & Owen S. (2007) 'Raise Your Game.' *Nursery World* 107 (4074).

Bolton, G. (2009*)* 'Write to Learn: Reflective Practice Writing.' *InnovAit* 2 (12).

Bronfenbrenner, U. (1994) 'Ecological Models of Human Development.' Available at www.psy.cmu.edu/~siegler/35bronfebrenner94.pdf (accessed March 2011).

Browne, N. (2008) *Gender Equity in the Early Years*. Maidenhead: OUP.

Clark, A. (2010) *Breaking Methodological Boundaries: Exploring Participatory Visual Methods*. Paper at EECERA 2010 Birmingham (Abstract Book).

Common Core (2010) Available at www.cwdcouncil.org.uk/common-core (accessed 23 March 2010).

Convery, A. (1998) 'A Teacher's Response to Reflection in Action.' *Cambridge Journal of Education* 28 (2). Available at http://dx.doi.org/10.1080/0305764980280205 (accessed February 2011).

CWDC (2008a) *Guidance to the Standards for the Award of Early Years Professional Status*. Leeds: CWDC.

CWDC (2008b) *On the Right Track: Guidance to the Standards for the Award of Early Years Professional Status*. Leeds: CWDC.

CWDC (2009) *Final Draft of Unit Promote Learning and Development in the Early Years, Level 3 Diploma for the Children and Young Peoples Workforce*. Leeds: CWDC.

Dahlberg, G., Moss, P. & Pence, A. (2003) *Beyond Quality in Early Childhood Education and Care*. London: RoutledgeFalmer.

Dalton, S. (2008) *Beyond Intellectual Blackmail: Foucault and Habermas on Reason, Truth, and Enlightenment E–Logos Electronic Journal for Philosophy*. Available at http://nb.vse.cz/kfil/elogos/history/dalton08.pdf (accessed April 2008).

DCSF (2008a) *The Early Years Foundation Stage*. Nottingham: DCSF.

DCSF (2008b) *Statutory Framework for the Early Years Foundation Stage*. Available at http://nationalstrategies.standards.dcsf.gov.uk/node/151379 (accessed April 2010).

DfE (2013) *More Great Childcare*. London: HM Government.

DfES (2005) *Common Core of Skills and Knowledge for the Children's Workforce*. Nottingham: DfES.

DfES (2007) *Early Years Foundation Stage*. Nottingham: DfES.

Drew, S. & Bingham, R. (2009) *The Guide to Learning and Study Skills*. Farnham: Gower.

Driscoll, J. (2000) *Practising Clinical Supervision: A Reflective Approach*. Oxford: Blackwell.

Every Child Matters (2010) Available at www.dcsf.gov.uk/everychildmatters/ (accessed August 2010).

Edwards, C., Gandini, L. & Forman, G. (1998) *The Hundred Languages of Children* (2nd ed). Westport, CT: Ablex.

Evans, M. (2011a) 'Explore the Value of Self-Reflection.' *Nursery World* 111 (4255).

Evans, M. (2011b) 'More Emphasis on Reflective Practice.' *Nursery World* 111 (4263).

Farrelly, P. (ed) (2010) *Early Years Work-Based Learning*. Exeter: Learning Matters.

Fisher, J. (2008) *Starting from the Child*. Maidenhead: OUP.

Fook, J. & Askeland, G. A. (2007) 'The "Critical" in Critical Reflection.' In S. White, J. Fook & F. Gardner (eds), *Critical Reflection in Health and Social Care*. Maidenhead: OUP.

Freire, P. (1975) *Pedagogy of the Oppressed*. Harmondsworth: Penguin.

Giardiello, P. & McNulty, J. (2009) 'Back to the Future of Early Childhood: Same but Different.' In W. Bignold & L. Gayton (eds), *Global Issues and Comparative Education*. Exeter: Learning Matters.

Gibbs, G. (1988) *Learning by Doing: A Guide to Teaching and Learning Methods*. Oxford: Oxford Brookes.

Gros, F. (2010) *The Government of Self and Others: Lectures at the College de France 1982–1983*. Basingstoke: Palgrave Macmillan.

Habermas, J. (1976) *Legitimation Crisis*. London: Heinemann.

Haralambos, M. & Holborn, M. (2004) *Sociology: Themes and Perspectives* (6th ed). London: Collins.

IQF (2010) Available at www.childrensworkforce.org.uk/workstreams/iqf/ (accessed 23 March 2013).

Kincheloe, J. & McClaren, P. (2005) 'Rethinking Critical Theory and Qualitative Research.' In N. Denzin & Y. Lincoln, *The SAGE Handbook of Qualitative Research* (3rd ed). Thousand Oaks, CA: SAGE.

Kolb, D. A. (1984) *Experiential Learning: Experience as a Source of Learning and Development.* Englewood Cliffs, NJ: Prentice Hall.

Leeson, C. (2004) 'In Praise of Reflective Practice.' In J. Willan, R. Parker-Rees & J. Savage (eds), *Early Childhood Studies.* Exeter: Learning Matters.

Lively, J. & Lively, A. (eds) (1994) *Democracy in Britain.* Oxford: Blackwell.

Mac Naughton, G. (2006) *Doing Foucault in Early Childhood Studies.* Abingdon: Routledge.

Mac Naughton, G. (2008) *Shaping Early Childhood.* Maidenhead: OUP.

Mezirow, J. and Associates (1990) *Fostering Critical Reflection in Adulthood.* San Francisco: Jossey-Bass.

Moon, J. (2003) *Learning Journals and Logs, Reflective Diaries.* UCD Dublin. Available at www.deakin.edu.au/itl/assets/resources/pd/tl-modules/teaching-approach/group-assignments/learning-journals.pdf (accessed April 2013).

Moon, J. (2008) *Critical Thinking: An Exploration of Theory and Practice.* London: Routledge.

Morrison, K. (1996) 'Developing Reflective Practice in Higher Degree Students through a Learning Journal.' *Studies in Higher Education* 21 (3).

Moss, P. (2008) 'Foreword'. In A. Paige-Smith & A. Craft, *Developing Reflective Practice in the Early Years.* Maidenhead: OUP.

Moss, P. (2010) 'We Cannot Continue as We Are: The Educator in an Education for Survival.' *Contemporary Issues in Early Childhood* 11 (1).

Nutbrown, C. (2012, June) *Foundations for Quality. The Independent Review of Early Education and Childcare Qualifications: Final Report.* Cheshire: DfE.

Nutbrown, C. & Abbott, L. (2001) 'Experiencing Reggio Emilia.' In L. Abbott & C. Nutbrown, *Experiencing Reggio Emilia.* Buckingham: OUP.

Osgood, J. (2010) 'Narrative Methods in the Nursery: (Re)-Considering Claims to Give Voice through Processes of Decision-Making.' *Reconceptualizing Educational Research Methodology* 1 (1).

Parker-Rees, R., Leeson, C., Willan, J. & Savage, J. (eds) (2010) *Early Childhood Studies* (3rd ed). Exeter: Learning Matters.

Petrie, P., Boddy, J., Cameron, C., Wigfall, V. & Simon, A. (2006) *Working with Children in Care: European Perspectives.* Maidenhead: OUP.

Rinaldi, C. (2005) *In Dialogue with Reggio Emilia.* London: Routledge.

Royle, N. (2003) *Jacques Derrida.* Abingdon: Routledge.

Scandinavian School (2010) Available at www.scandinavianschool.org/about_school/reggio_emilia.htm (accessed June 2010).

Schofield, R. (2009) 'Growing the Learner from Within: Deep Learning through Experiential and Reflective Events.' *International Journal of Mentoring and Coaching* 2 (2).

Schön, D. (1983) *The Reflective Practitioner.* London: Temple Smith.

Smith, G. & Nicolson, P. (2011) 'Despair? . . . Older Homeless Men's Accounts of Their Emotional Trajectories.' *Oral History* 39 (1).

Smythe, J. (1989) 'Developing and Sustaining Critical Reflection in Teacher Education.' *Journal of Teacher Education* 40 (1).

Thompson, S. & Thompson, N. (2008) *The Critically Reflective Practitioner.* Basingstoke: Palgrave.

Tindal, I. (2006) *Discovering Reflective Practice*. Available at http://firstclass.ultraversity.net/~ian.
tindal/rm/modeloverview.html (accessed 24 November 2009).

UNCRC (2010) Available at www.unicef.org/crc/ (accessed August 2010).

Urban, M. (2008) 'Dealing with Uncertainty: Challenges and Possibilities for the Early Years
Profession.' *European Early Childhood Education Research Journal* 16 (2).

Whalley, M. (2008) *Leading Practice in Early Years Settings*. Exeter: Learning Matters.

White, S. (2007) 'Unsettling Reflections: The Reflexive Practitioner as "Trickster" in Interprofessional Work.' In S. White, J. Fook & F. Gardner (eds), *Critical Reflection in Health and Social
Care*. Maidenhead: OUP.

Wilkinson, J. (1996) 'Definition of Reflective Practice.' In S. Hinchliff (ed), *Dictionary of Nursing* (17th ed). Edinburgh: Churchill Livingstone.

Chapter 7

The student practitioner constructing a professional identity

Ruby Oates

By the end of this chapter you will:

- Place the development of the early childhood education and care workforce in a historical, cultural and political context.
- Appreciate the current policy background in relation to efforts to professionalise the early childhood education and care workforce.
- Consider research on early childhood practitioners' experiences in the workplace, education and training.
- Recognise different constructions and discourses on professionalism and consider how feminist, post-structural theories challenge traditional and contemporary discourses on the role of practitioners in the early childhood workforce.
- Move forward as an early childhood studies graduate to reflect critically upon your own personal and professional development to enhance your employability, practice and career progression.

Introduction

This chapter allows you to build upon your academic studies in early childhood and your developing practice and emerging critical insight and thinking. It explores the background to the recent attempts in England and Wales to professionalise the early childhood workforce, discusses what constitutes an early childhood professional and places this discussion within a historical, cultural, political and social policy context. It incorporates a discussion on contemporary discourses on early childhood professionalism and considers recent research evidence relating to the childcare workforce's experiences of the sector and efforts to professionalise it. This provides readers with an opportunity to use this chapter as a platform from which to consider and reflect upon their own personal and professional development.

Placing the development of the early childhood and care workforce in historical, cultural and political contexts

The position of the overwhelmingly female childcare workforce in the UK (Cameron *et al.* 2001; DfE 2012) has, until recently, received little attention in terms of academic study and research, reflecting the status of women's work and the lack of value given to care work in general.

Randall (2000), in exploring the historical development of childcare in Britain, notes how the care and education of younger children was viewed very differently from that of older children. Randall suggests that the landmark 1870 Education Act (Randall 2000:21) signified the government's recognition of the need for universal elementary education and an acceptance that the state would play a part in its provision. This reflects the emergence of a romantic and evangelical thinking about children and childhood, moving from an earlier nineteenth-century discourse focusing on children's delinquency and behaviour. Likewise, Hendricks (cited in James & Prout 1997:44) says that at the heart of the Education Acts of the 1870s and 1880s was a particular construction of an 'innocent' child who needed protection.

Mayall (2002) suggests that children encountered a raw deal at the hands of policymakers during the following century, particularly so when compared with other European countries which provided universal, high-quality state-run nurseries. British preschool children were the 'victims of a ramshackle patchwork of poor services' (Mayall, 2002:13). She identifies in particular the work of Qvortrup (1991), James and Prout (1997) and Hendrick (1994, 1997) as significant during the latter part of the twentieth century, in shifting ideas about children's rights and needs through the provision of a sociological discourse.

Pugh (2001, with Duffy 2006) notes how successive governments supported the principles of nursery education but seldom found resources to fund it. This saw the emergence of two parallel developments: one, the emergence of a voluntary sector during the 1960s, and two, the growth during the 1990s of private sector day care for the very young. Pugh (2001:10) notes, 'This legacy is important in understanding the state of early childhood services at the beginning of the twenty-first century. A review in 1988 found a patchwork of fragmented and uncoordinated services.'

Lewis (2003) suggests that the Labour government's National Childcare Strategy (DfEE 1998) represented a profound shift in thinking through its focus on the education rather than care of very young children. This change was radical in the sense that successive post-war governments had assumed childcare would remain the responsibility of mothers, supported by wider family members. Yet while policies have attempted to direct women into work, the actual childcare system intended to promote this policy has changed little, with no departure from a mixed economy of care. Lewis (2003:223) notes, 'The old distinction between nursery education and childcare has been formally extinguished only in the new administrative arrangements. The position in respect of funding and provision is much more blurred, and crucially, in respect of staffing, remains very divided.'

Brannen and Moss (2003) suggest that the development of childcare reflects a set of power relationships between men and women, and includes a gender hierarchy and division of labour. Moss (in Brannen & Moss 2003) notes three components:

one, a norm of individualised care within the family distinguishing between the private family and public provision; two, the creation of a gender regime through which a powerful ideology of motherhood exercises considerable influence; and three, a socio-economic imperative linked to the eradication of poverty and the need for a competitive workforce. Moss suggests that the liberal state now finds itself intervening to an unparalleled extent into the private world of the family, as childcare is now the subject of public policy, but its responsibility and practice remain in the private domain. This reinforces and perpetuates a gender regime whereby maternalism is provided by substitute mothers through a childcare workforce that is overwhelmingly female, with often poor pay and working conditions with a low qualifications base.

Moss questions what he sees as a narrow, instrumental and dominant understanding of childcare. He suggests childcare need not be a replication of the home; it could be a space where young children are viewed as active subject with rights, voices and a network of relationships (for more see Moss & Petrie 2002), a place where care moves from being a tradable commodity to being seen as an ethic. Moss notes (in Brannen & Moss 2003:39), 'Care as ethic moves us from care as a task performed by adults on children. Rather care is inscribed in all relationships. Adults *and* [author's emphasis] children care and express this care in all relationships in the early childhood institution.'

Small group or individual activity

- Consider how the historical separation of education and care in Britain shapes childcare provision today.
- Do you believe a gender regime exists in the childcare setting? What keeps it in place?
- What do you think Moss means when he talks of '*care as ethic*'?
- How might childcare provision incorporate an ethic of care and what does it look like? Share and discuss your comments with others.

The policy background between 1997 and 2013

Owen and Hayes (in Miller & Cable 2012) note how early years services in the UK lacked any policy direction until the Labour government in 1997–1998 developed a National Childcare Strategy (DfEE 1998). This included, for the first time, free part-time nursery education to all four-year-olds and, later, three-year-old children. Two factors appear important in its emergence: one, social policies addressing social exclusion and where possible, providing parents with opportunities to join the workforce; and two, a serious child protection issues and the subsequent Laming report (Laming 2003). These factors highlighted the importance of the early childhood workforce in terms of the eventual successes of these policies. At the same time early childhood academics (for example, Abbott & Pugh 1998) played a small but important part in influencing government policies in some respects, initially in terms of concerns about the quality of the workforce. Of particular importance was the government consultation strategy (DfES 2005, 2006a) on the childcare workforce which led to the eventual development of a new role in childcare – that is, the Early Years Professional Status (EYPS), and the promise of the development of an integrated qualifications framework across the sector (DfES 2006b).

Early childhood academics, including those involved in the delivery of early childhood studies specialist degrees, were disappointed with the then government's response (see, in particular, Calder in Miller & Cable 2012). Calder, the chair of the Early Childhood Studies Degree Network in the UK, notes this was a lost opportunity to create a new graduate pedagogic role within the field of early childhood education and care, with graduates from the early childhood studies degrees moving into postgraduate training:

> We believe that either a 'new' teacher or pedagogue model would be a necessary step forward to help raise the quality of early years' provision. We believe this could be achieved by developing a new postgraduate certificate along the lines of the existing PGCE . . . it should carry a regulated status.
>
> (Calder 2006)

My own research (Oates 2011) tracking early childhood studies graduates who are experienced practitioners, between 2007 and 2009 from across five counties in the East Midlands, found many positives about working in the sector, particularly in relation to practitioners' enjoyment, love and passion for their work with young children. However, it also found anger, confusion and misunderstanding about lack of value given to their role and frustration regarding the frequency of qualification and status changes, which many practitioners saw as undermining their hard work and higher education studies.

The coalition government formed in 2010 instigated yet another review of early education and childcare qualifications. In its final report (DfE 2012) Nutbrown recommended, among other things, the creation of a new early years' specialist route to Qualified Teacher Status (QTS), specialising from birth to seven.

> An early years' teacher will need to demonstrate the same skills and meet the same standards as are required by any other teacher. I think of an early years' teacher as being 'specialist' in early childhood development, play and learning as elsewhere a teacher might be 'specialist' in a particular curriculum subject.
>
> (DfE 2012:58)

However, while the government (DfE 2013:27) accepted graduate leadership as the best way to improve outcomes for young children, it created a new role, the Early Years Teacher, yet rejected the recommended by Nutbrown to attach Qualified Teacher Status (QTS) to it. For Nutbrown (2013) and many in the sector, myself included, this is very disappointing as it is seen as a continuing devaluation of early years pedagogy and the status of those who work with the under-fives. Nutbrown (2013: 10), the author of the review, in a highly critical response to the rejection of QTS to the role, suggests it is 'the watering down of good quality qualifications, and the implementing of a two-tier status for teachers.'

We can see, then, that childcare work has been subject to many influences and policy changes over many years, and the following section focuses on the research evidence in relation to practitioners' experiences in the sector.

Research findings on early childhood practitioners' experiences of the workplace, education and training

Early childhood academics, and pressure groups on behalf of young children, have consistently argued for better training and development opportunities in the sector (see, for example, NCB 1992; Abbott & Pugh 1998; Boddy *et al.* 2005; Miller & Cable 2012). The previous government's National Childcare Strategy (DfEE 1998) and its efforts to tackle social deprivation alongside a focus on safeguarding children through the Every Childhood Matters (DfES 2003) outcomes have led to an increased interest in the quality of early childhood education and care and, as recognised in the previous section, the promotion of a professionalisation agenda in the workforce.

Three large-scale studies provide insight into the childcare workforce during the latter part of the last century and early part of this century. Cameron *et al.*'s (2001) study on the entry, retention and loss of childcare workers in the private sector used Labour Force Survey data from 1996–1998 alongside findings from a national survey on childcare courses, plus a survey of 2,000 day nursery heads and other staff working in registered day nurseries. This sample was made up of 2,060 staff from 251 nurseries in sixteen local authorities, and six focus groups from various regions were also held. The combined findings suggest strengths in the workforce are the particularly high degree of commitment to childcare work, practitioners' passion and the job satisfaction. However, concerns expressed by both staff and students related to difficulties in developing a career, the low pay and the challenges for workers to manage work and their own personal caring responsibilities. Workers repeatedly claimed that their work is not valued, and the key factor for this is their low pay.

Sylva *et al.*'s (2004) study was used by the government at the time to justify the need for workforce reform, leading to a professionalisation agenda (DfES 2006a), and was the first major European longitudinal study of young children's development between the ages of three to seven years. It is a significant study because it is the first large-scale one in this country to suggest that there is a link between the quality of provision in preschool education and positive outcomes for children.

A more recent report exploring pay, progression and professionalisation in the childcare workforce was undertaken by Cooke and Lawton (2008). The aim of this report was to investigate how low wages and limited progression opportunities played out in the workforce. Their methodology included eight focus groups and included fifty-three practitioners in four towns across the east of England in late 2007. Their findings note that all participants earned less than £6.67 per hour, putting this group in a low-pay threshold. The average age of the participant was thirty-two years, and the sample included only one male worker.

The report (Cooke & Lawton 2008) concludes that low pay, low status and a high proportion of females in the workforce interact and reinforce with one another, having a knock-on effect upon recruitment and retention of staff. It notes that only 7 per cent of those working in full day care have post-secondary school qualifications. In commenting upon the impact of the professionalising agenda by the then Labour government, it notes contradictory views across the workforce, ranging from frustration that pay is not matched with responsibility and status and a resistance from some workers to the hallmarks of professionalism such as qualifications. They found entrenched professional divisions between early years' workers and other children services professionals, alongside a sense of powerlessness among workers that changes are being done to them rather than in partnership with them.

My own research (Oates 2011) supports these findings, suggesting the micro-politics of the early childhood setting is a place where many practitioners experience limited power to effect change. However, it is pleasing to note that in the second national survey of practitioners with Early Years Professional Status (EYPS), Hadfield and Jopling (2012) found widespread belief among Early Years Practitioners that gaining the EYPS had improved their career prospects. The report also notes that the main barrier to career progression and mobility was low pay, and the survey found that 71 per cent of the participants earned less than £25,000 per annum; this was less than the average weekly pay for the UK (Hadfield & Jopling 2012:42) as a whole in September 2011. The issue of low pay, therefore, continues to be one of the key concerns for practitioners working in the sector and has been so for some time, as reinforced by the findings presented in this chapter.

Individual and group activity: use findings from large-scale research studies to consider your own experiences of the sector

- With others discuss, in an ethical manner, how the research findings here relate to your own experiences of the sector either as a student-practitioner and/or experienced practitioner.
- As a group, identify how the different policies have and continue to affect the workforce, in particular efforts by governments to professionalise it.
- As a group, agree what works and what is to be done to ensure the workforce is fit for its purpose.

Smaller-scale studies tend to reinforce findings from larger-scale studies, though their emphasis is often different. Robins and Silcock (2001) explored how English nursery nurses in schools talked about their jobs. They suggest that the organizational split between education and childcare means that status differences tend to be more pronounced in the early childhood workforce, leading to nursery nurses being grouped alongside parents as helpers in school. The job title itself identifies nursery nurses as carers, reflecting the health and welfare discourse through which its title emerged (for more on the historical development of childcare in the UK, see Randall 2000; Mayall 2002; and Lewis 2003).

There is some earlier evidence (see Bertram & Pascal 1995; Carlson & Karp 1997) that nursery nurses have had some success in establishing their credibility as a profession, particularly in relation to their effective practical skills and the key role they play in supporting inclusion for children with additional needs. However, Cleave and Brown (1991) and Mansell (1993) found that nursery nurses perceive themselves as low-status and invisible in the workplace in part because of the way other professionals treat them. One of the key findings of my own research (Oates 2011) reinforced this finding, as can be seen in the following comment by one practitioner/participant:

> It is being ordered around and quite often that can involve being ordered away from a child you are there to support and sent to do the photo-copying which I don't think is the same magnitude really.
> (Teaching assistant, fourteen years' experience, from Oates 2011)

Discourses on professionalism: how feminist, post-structural perspectives challenge traditional and contemporary discourses

Sociologists and others, over many decades, have attempted to define what constitutes a professional and a profession. Evetts (2003, 2006) suggests that there are two main models of what constitutes a profession; she refers to them as an Anglo-American model and a European model. European professionals, she suggests, have differed from their self-employed Anglo-American counterparts in being employees of public services or government bureaucracies. Gleeson and Knights (2006) note two contrasting discourses on professionalism dominant within sociology. One is a discourse that focuses on the structures in which professionals work; in this scenario professionals are subject to external rules and constraints with a particular focus over recent years on audit, regulation, management and inspection. Another discourse focuses on the individual agency of professionals and the ways in which they construct meaning and identity in their roles, therefore seeing an active professional rather than a professional who is constrained by regulation and control.

Recent government policies of modernisation, Gleeson and Knights (2006:29) suggest, have sought to upskill individuals in both the private and public sectors of the economy, thus bringing into question the traditional assumption about the municipal profession as a 'trusted civic authority'. They suggest there has been a major shift from professionalism towards professionality. They argue that professionalism contains assumptions about the work organization, managerialism, inspection and audit, while by contrast, professionality implies a new authority finding expression in changes in identity, enterprise and self-regulation. They suggest this can be seen in the current debates surrounding public sector professionals such as nurses, where a strong market and managerial discourse is potentially having the effect of de-professionalising and casualizing professional practice. Gleeson and Knights (2006) suggest that today few professions have been able to avoid the erosion of their independence from employers, organizations or the state as industrial growth, globalization and an expansion of governmental interventions have occurred.

Public sector professionals such as teachers, however, have never been in a position to define the relationship between themselves and the public because of the existence of the state as their employer, a situation very different from, for example, self-employed lawyers. However, this inability of public sector professionals to define the relationship between the provider and consumer of professional service does not mean that everyone is of the same status. Other factors such as hierarchy, gender, levels of pay, training and status ensure that certain groups remain subordinate, as demonstrated in research on nursery nurses and early childhood practitioners; see, for example, Cooke and Lawton (2008) and Oates (2011).

Many writers from other disciplines have noted a deskilling of professional roles, including a loss of autonomy; for example, the medical profession (Haug 1988), the public sector (Exworthy & Halford 1999) and social work (Allen 2003). Moriarty's (2000) comparative study of teachers in England and Finland is particularly useful. She found that English teachers are now more likely to see themselves as technicians rather than as autonomous professionals because of the ways in which their roles are centrally prescribed and regulated by government. In many ways this can be seen in the position of early childhood practitioners in the workforce, who have, in recent years, been subject to an imposed professionalisation by governments, as identified earlier in this chapter.

Individual and group activity: what is a profession?

- In your own time, find a definition of the words 'profession' and 'professionalism'.
- As a small group, agree upon a set of criteria which you could use to make an assessment as to whether a particular occupational group is a profession.
- As a large group, discuss how the different definitions help or hinder an understanding of the early childhood education and care workforce as a profession.

The emergence of feminist discourses on professionalism

Feminist writers such as Crompton (1987), Witz (1992), Bottero (1992), Davies (1996) and Oakley (2005) have examined women's growing entry into areas of professional work over a number of years and noted the invisibility of women's experience in the workplace and in research within traditional sociology and management studies. Of particular note is Davies's (1996) discussion on the sociology of professions and the profession of gender. Davies explores the idea of democratic professionalism yet incorporates and addresses wider principles of equity and social justice through a gender analysis of organizations. She suggests that within sociology there has been a shift away from regarding gender as an attribute towards viewing it as a relation, something that is socially constructed and not fixed:

> Regarding gender as an active and continuing process and carrying out gender relations analysis in this way is often signalled by a shift from using gender as a noun to using gender as a verb. Thus, it becomes possible to speak of the 'gendering' of organisations and the 'gendered' character of policies and organisation activities.
>
> (Davies 1996:664)

Viewing gender in this way is problematic because of the way it blurs the distinction between men/masculinity and women/femininity and the consequent power attached to gender roles in society. Davies suggests that a way round this is to view gender not as something directly related to the behaviour of men and women but as one cultural resource, among many, that can be called upon in the process of 'creating and sustaining identities, utilised in daily interaction, available as image and metaphor in the shaping of organisation and institutional arrangements' (Davies 1996:665).

What we should be doing, she suggests, is taking into account the ways in which sexual difference structures our social relations and signifies power and status, rather than reducing gender to behaviour differences. This view is developed through an exploration of how, historically, men were the key actors in organizations and bureaucracies and the values embedded in the notion of the practice of a profession reflected a 'masculine project and repressing or denying those qualities culturally assigned to femininity' (Davies 1996:669).

Individual and group activity: the gendering of organizations

- Consider your own experiences in different organizations in terms of how they are 'gendered'.
- With others and through a gender analysis, discuss in an ethical manner the ways in which childcare settings are gendered and the impact of this on the values and practice in the workplace.
- In your discussion, consider the ways om which gender is culturally constructed and how this shapes our understandings of early years' professionals and the roles men and women play within this workforce.

Davies suggests that the occupational cultures in Britain were directly drawn from ideologies of gender and gender imagery to explain the relations between the 'professional work of men and the "supportive" activities of women' (Davies 1996:669). She suggests that professional judgement is based on autonomy and detachment devoid of emotion; the ideal typical professional encounter is one that privileges male characteristics while denigrating or suppressing female ones. This is an important distinction as many early years' writers (Manning-Morton 2006; Moyles 2001; Moss 2006; Osgood 2006a) emphasise the importance of incorporating a relational dimension into a construction of an early childhood professional identity.

Davies, writing before an early years' professionalisation agenda was in place in the UK, notes how in the fields of health, welfare and education, issues related to professional transformation, where new market philosophies and forms of managerialism have presented particularly effective challenges to professional hegemony, have coincided with a feminisation of the workforce.

A number of feminist readings on the position of women in the childcare draw upon the ideas of Bourdieu and Foucault. See, for example, how Colley (2006) applies Bourdieusian concepts and how Skeggs (1988), Reay (2000) and Mac Naughton (2005) apply Foucauldian concepts to provide a feminist understanding of childcare work.

Of particular early influence is the work of Bates (1990, 1991, 1994), who provides a feminist, post-structural analysis of women's entry into the workforce. She finds this entry may constitute a discrete phase of social reproduction within specific occupational cultures which bind the broader influences of class and gender. Bates applies Foucault's (1977) ideas in relation to how technology, in this instance vocational training, is used to discipline and control the workforce in neo-liberal societies.

Bates's study of 'care girls' who work in residential care homes for older people found a concern about the 'interface between cultural resources acquired through family experience and the process of becoming a care assistant through YTS' (Bates 1991:234). Her study notes how vocational training in the workplace is not confined to the official project of developing skills; it operates more covertly through social processes involved in screening, disciplining and socially constructing specific skills and dispositions in the 'care girls':

> Working class girls, particularly those whose family life has exposed them to experiences such as care of the young or elderly, crowded conditions, demanding physical work, verbal and physical aggression and related psychological stress would appear to be the ideal candidates.
>
> (Bates 1991:234)

Bates draws upon Foucault's (1977) disciplinary technologies – in particular the role of surveillance as a coercive means of observation. For the 'care girls' their surveillance occurs through the vocational training as a means of occupational socialization whereby surveillance is normalised and legitimized in the name of training, suggesting that work entry is 'thus located within tighter frameworks of social control' (Bates 1991:235). In this scenario there is much to be gained from obedience because conformity to the employers' expectations may lead to employment. Bates notes at the heart of this system is a competency-based framework curriculum module of training resulting from the employers' involvement in defining a specific set of competencies together with the grading of the trainees' achievement or failure. Bates (1991:237) argues, 'Thus competence-based learning coupled with new technology, in Foucault's terms, lowered the threshold of describable individuality and makes of this description a means of control and method of domination.'

Given the attention many feminists have given Foucault's ideas, they are worthy of further acknowledgement here. Foucault (cited in Dreyfus & Rabinow 1982) charts the growth since the sixteenth century of a new political form of power – namely, the state:

> . . . the state's power (and that's one of the reasons for its strength) is both an individualizing and a totalising form of power. Never, I think, in the history of human societies – even the old Chinese society – has there been such a tricky combination in the same political structures of individualization techniques, and of totalization procedures.
>
> (Foucault cited in Dreyfus & Rabinow 1982:213)

Power, he argues, designates a relationship between partners and creates blocks of 'regulated and concerted systems of power' (Dreyfus & Rabinow 1982:218). For

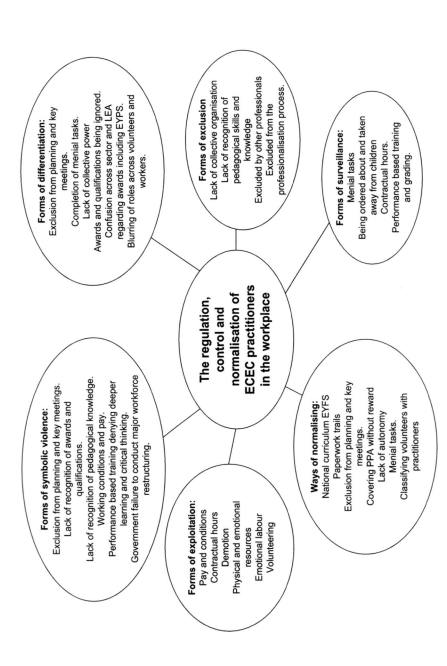

Forms of differentiation:
Exclusion from planning and key meetings.
Completion of menial tasks.
Lack of collective power
Awards and qualifications being ignored.
Confusion across sector and LEA regarding awards including EYPS.
Blurring of roles across volunteers and workers.

Forms of exclusion
Lack of collective organisation
Lack of recognition of pedagogical skills and knowledge
Excluded by other professionals
Excluded from the professionalisation process.

Forms of surveillance:
Menial tasks
Being ordered about and taken away from children
Contractual hours.
Performance based training and grading.

The regulation, control and normalisation of ECEC practitioners in the workplace

Forms of symbolic violence:
Exclusion from planning and key meetings.
Lack of recognition of awards and qualifications.
Lack of recognition of pedagogical knowledge.
Working conditions and pay.
Performance based training denying deeper learning and critical thinking.
Government failure to conduct major workforce restructuring.

Forms of exploitation:
Pay and conditions
Contractual hours
Demotion
Physical and emotional resources
Emotional labour
Volunteering

Ways of normalising:
National curriculum EYFS
Paperwork trails
Exclusion from planning and key meetings.
Covering PPA without reward
Lack of autonomy
Menial tasks.
Classifying volunteers with practitioners

Figure 7.1 The regulation, control and normalisation of ECEC practitioners in the workplace

example, in education institutions the blocks include such things as the different activities in lessons; codes of obedience; differentiating pupils through classes and grades; marking individuals out through surveillance, enclosure, attendance, punishment, hierarchies, rules, rewards and regulated procedures.

Foucault notes that power relations in society have been progressively governmentalized through forms of rationalisation and centralisation under the auspices of state institutions and through a variety of disciplinary technologies. He argues that disciplinary power produces a human being that is docile yet productive, and he notes the usefulness of this in relation to the rise of capitalism. Foucault contends that it was the disciplinary technologies which underlay, but did not necessarily determine, the growth and triumph of capitalism as an economic venture. Foucault (1977) says that docile bodies are created through a process of subjectification, the aim of disciplinary technology being to forge a 'docile body that may be subjected, used, transformed and improved' (Foucault 1977:136), using technologies that include surveillance, exclusion, classification, distribution, individualisation, totalisation, regulation and normalisation. It is through these processes, Foucault argues, that the capacity exists to identify, measure, instil and regulate the behaviour of others.

My own research (Oates 2011) found practitioners subject to a range of disciplinary technologies used to keep them in their place in the hierarchy of the childcare setting, and examples of these can be seen in Figure 7.1.

Activity: applying post-structural concepts

- Foucault's theory is, in essence, a theory about the micro-politics of power in terms of how individual relate to one another. How might the micro-politics of power play out in early childhood settings?
- What disciplinary technologies regulate and control you, as a student or experienced practitioner, in your setting? Be mindful of ethical practice when discussing with others and places of work.
- Why may there be reluctance from other professionals to acknowledge practitioners' pedagogical skills and the knowledge of early childhood practitioners?
- Does the balance of power need to change? Can and how might it?

The significant influences of Foucauldian and Bourdieusian concepts are acknowledged as particularly important in the writing of contemporary writers applying feminist, postmodern and post-structuralist concepts and perspectives. The Bourdieusian concepts of habitus, capitals and field provide opportunities for feminists to explore the social reproduction of women in the workplace through vocational training (for more, see Colley et al. 2003) and how a gendered regime may be perpetuated, while the Foucauldian concept of disciplinary technologies provides us with tools to explore the micro-politics of the workplace for early childhood care and education workers.

What is an early childhood professional?

Oberheumer (cited in Miller & Cable 2012) asks what an early years' professional is. She notes how, over the past decade in many parts of Europe, the topic of early childhood education and care has received a new and more visible status on the policy agenda of many countries; she notes evidence from the Organisation for Economic and Co-operative Development (OECD 2001, 2006) and Neuman (2005) of this trend (see Oberheumer in Miller & Cable 2012:131). Many countries, she suggests, are grappling with the question of what an early childhood professional is. Oberheumer (in Miller & Cable 2012:137) argues that the varying policies around the world reflect culturally embedded understandings of the role of early childhood institutions and those who work within them. In turn, she believes these shape the images early childhood practitioners have of themselves. She notes the differences between the pre-primary specialist rooted in public education and the early childhood pedagogues who possess broader-based, more socio-pedagogical understandings of care, learning, education and upbringing. It is her view that this latter understanding of the professional role signifies the way forward. Oberheumer (2007:138) concludes,

> However, this is an ambitious model. It requires not only critical thinking and analytic, collaborative dispositions and skills, but also new societal understandings of professional pedagogical-education work with young children, new approaches towards valuing that work, and new policy commitments regarding the available resources for supporting this work.

Individual and group activity: rethinking professionalism – what is an early childhood professional?

- On your own, list the qualities that you would expect to find in an early childhood professional.
- As a small group, come to a consensus about what qualities you would expect to find in an early childhood professional.
- As a large group discuss your findings and consider how your definitions compare to traditional ideas of what constitutes a professional.

Dalli's (cited in Miller & Cable 2012) recent work also confirms that beyond Europe, many countries are grappling with the concept of an early childhood professional. Dalli discusses how New Zealand is making real efforts to professionalise the early childhood workforce through a graduate lead profession. Dalli (cited in Miller & Cable 2012:147) notes how in New Zealand they started by 'articulating a ground-up definition of professionalism that would sit comfortably across the different types of early childhood services in New Zealand.' This definition is based around three major themes, which she says emerged as key components of teachers' perspectives on the nature of professional behaviour:

1. Pedagogy – strategies and styles: This includes listening to children, not imposing adults' agenda on them, not singling out children for special attention. Strategies

also include planning, scaffolding, reflecting on practice as markers of professionalism (Dalli cited in Miller & Cable: 2012:147).

2. Professional knowledge and practice: This included being knowledgeable about children and theories of early childhood as a starting point for professional practice and an ability to be a reflective practitioner willing to critique and improve one's own practice (Dalli cited in Miller & Cable 2012:148–149).

3. Collaborative relationships: Dalli (cited in Miller & Cable 2012:149) notes one of the three main goals of New Zealand's ten-year strategy is promoting collaborative partnerships. This means working together, being respectful and supportive of colleagues, working in partnership with them, modelling a cooperative approach and consulting with other professionals. Collaborative relationships naturally include working with parents in a way that encourages them to work collaboratively with practitioners.

Individual activity: your interpretation of early childhood professionalism

- Using Dalli's three themes cited here, consider how these relate to your own interpretation of professional practice and professionalism.
- Read Dalli's (in Miller & Cable 2012) work in full and consider how these strategies and ideas apply to your own experience in settings as a student-practitioner / experienced practitioner.
- Ask yourself, how do these strategies inform your own ideas about what an early childhood professional should be?

For an interesting review of New Zealand's early childhood education policy and the concept of a critical ecology of the early childhood profession, read Dalli (2010).

Debates about what constitutes an early childhood professional have led many academics in the UK to share their concerns about recent government efforts to professionalise the early childhood workforce. Moss and Petrie (2002) suggest that early years' workers, including teachers, are becoming 'technicians' as opposed to professionals. Technicians, they suggest, focus on technical elements related to objective measurement, leading to a form of vulgar pragmatism, while professionals have autonomy and space to reflect on their practice using a critical pragmatism. They suggest a different approach whereby children are no longer seen as passive dependents of adults and services but as rich, competent, powerful, strong human beings. Further, Moss (2006) proposes some useful and critical questions about the images held of the early years' worker, and he questions what and who we understand the early years' worker to be. He suggests that there are three possible understandings or discourses about the worker. In one discourse, the worker is seen as the substitute mother, linking care work with motherhood and producing a gendered discourse. In this discourse there is an assumption that women have an innate capacity through their maternal instinct to play this role. A second discourse, that of the worker as a technician, is now more prominent because it better suits the marketplace 'through regulated processes to produce pre-specified and measurable outcomes'

(Moss 2006:35). The technician, he suggests, is inscribed with certain values, including certainty, as a result of outcomes that are known and measurable and through objectivity based upon a belief in the possibility of applying processes in a detached, objective way. An example from practice that some of you might identify with is the recent focus on the testing of younger children. England, he suggests, provides a clear example of the early years' worker as a technician:

> Technician status is most clearly seen in the approach to workforce education, an industrial-vocational system of workplace-based competency training and awards. 'Childcare' is viewed as an industry, whose employees . . . need to achieve industry defined National Occupational Standards, which are statements of the skills, knowledge and understanding required in a particular industry and clearly define the criteria for assessing competent performance.
>
> (Moss 2006:35)

Moss's third discourse is that of the worker as a researcher, an example of which can be found in the early childhood services in the Italian city of Reggio Emilia. The notion of the researching worker is based on the Vygotskyian idea of children as co-constructors with adults of knowledge. This worker, he argues, is a reflective and dialogic practitioner, whose work depends on relationships and the ability to listen and engage in dialogue, and, rather than pursuing conformity, the worker as researcher is open to new, unexpected ideas and uncertainty.

Osgood (2006b, and cited in Wood 2008) suggests that the current climate offers potential for an overhaul of early childhood provision, yet she fears this is tempered by economic rationalism; she argues that within this dominant discourse, professionals are constructed as the solution to society's ills, which places enormous responsibility on those who work with children. Her contribution is underpinned by the concepts of Foucault suggesting that the state plays a part in controlling, through its policies and structures, the behaviour of the workforce through the creation of a docile professional:

> Like school teachers, early years' practitioners now have to wrestle with the demands for accountability, attainment targets, a compulsory early years' curriculum and standardised approaches to their practice. All of which mark a sharp movement towards centralised control and prescription, which poses a potential threat to professional autonomy and morale.
>
> (Osgood cited in Wood 2008:272)

This questioning of dominant, masculine discourses about professionalism and questions about the emotional aspects of working with children and how this challenges existing ideas of being a professional have been explored by others, including the role of gender and social class, and these play a part in constructing an early years' workforce and practitioners' experiences of it. Cameron (2006), for example, emphasises the gendered nature of the workforce and proposes a construction of professionalism built on democratic ideas that provides a space for male and female workers. Brownhill's (2011) research into males working the 0–8 years sector provides interesting insight into the roles men are expected to play, such as being a father figure, the sporty one and a male role model, while Reay (2000) and Colley *et al.* (2003) note how working-class girls in particular are screened and sifted into care work.

Colley *et al.* (2003), using Bourdieu's notion of capitals (Bourdieu 1986), explore the emotional capital young working-class women put into their work. They suggest that care courses such as nursery nursing socialise and discipline students into fulfilling the role of carers for the benefit of middle-class parents. They note how young women who resist this socialisation during their childcare training are soon excluded from the courses. They suggest that the raw materials on which these girls learn to labour is themselves – that is, successful trainees possess particular dispositions; successful students, therefore, have to work on their own feelings in order to learn to labour appropriately and fit into the habitus of the childcare setting. Colley *et al.* (2003:477) introduce the term 'vocational habitus' to explain how students are oriented towards a particular set of dispositions which relate to gender, family background and location within the working class in order to develop a specific type of worker that meets the needs of the workplace.

My own research findings (Oates 2011) suggest that a gender regime is reinforced further through the way in which mothers volunteer in their children's schools; this perpetuates the linking of childcare work with motherhood and women's maternal role in society. This can lead to a blurring of the roles of volunteer and the nursery nurse, and in so doing may undermine the value and status of the role of ECEC workers and perpetuate a view that working with young children does not require specialist skills, attributes, abilities and knowledge.

A very different but equally as important discourse is presented by Penn (2007, 2011), who provides a critical account of the management of the childcare market. Her examination focuses on the growth of corporate childcare, which she notes has increased sevenfold since 1997 (Penn 2007). While her position is not directly related to the professionalisation of the early years' workforce, her contribution provides insight into the economic and structural contexts and conditions in which professionalisation takes place. This is useful because it reminds us of the structures through which an early childhood professional identity will emerge.

Penn presents a critique about the increasing privatisation of childcare provision in the UK. She suggests that early education and care has always been a 'marginal state service' (Penn 2007:193), and in charting the background to recent government policies, she argues that the Labour government made no real inroads to the traditions it inherited from the Conservative government because to have done so would have 'challeng[ed] vested interests' (Penn 2007:198). Penn suggests that governments have actively encouraged private sector engagement in spite of concerns about the quality of provision, citing sixteen companies now providing 50,000 childcare places in the private sector. Penn (2007:204) notes, 'What is so striking about the current situation in early education and care in the United Kingdom is the absence of public concern or information about the expansion that has taken place.'

Penn's insight into the economic and structural conditions in which professionalisation will take place raises some serious concerns about the conditions and context in which professionalisation of the early childhood workforce will take place.

Individual and group activity: the privatisation of early childhood work

- In your own time, explore the providers of childcare outside the family in your locality.
- What does Penn (2007:193) mean when she talks about early education and care being a 'marginal state service' and why is this?
- To whom does she refer when she talks about 'challenging vested interests'? (Penn 2007:198).
- While Penn talks about the absence of public concern about what has taken place, does electronic media have the potential to change the discourses around early childhood education and care and its provision?

There is some evidence that social media is having an impact upon contemporary discourses about early childhood education and care, its practice and provision, thus widening debates about the provision of childcare to include the voices of parents and practitioners. A good example of this is the way in which parents' concerns about the proposed decrease in child/staff ratio (DfE 2013:29–33) have led to a reversal of this proposal by the coalition government (see *Independent* 2013). It does seem that the power of parents' voices and of those working in the sector, through social media – for example, the impact of website campaigns led by the educational charity the Pre-school Learning Alliance and Mumsnet (2013) to generate a debate about child/staff ratios and achieve a reversal of government policy – may indeed provide new opportunities for a wider section of the community to take part in debates about childcare provision in this country and across the world.

Chapter summary: constructing your own professional identity

This chapter has brought together many of the key themes of this book, through an exploration of how early childhood education and care have developed and changed over many years. It has noted the historical, political and cultural contexts in which this workforce developed alongside the different influences that have shaped its current position and construction.

It is, however, still early days in the UK in terms of the development of the early childhood workforce as a profession. It is evident that early childhood education and care has been, and will remain, subject to various political, economic and educational pressures involving a complex range of interest groups with power imbalances. However, the more graduate early childhood specialists enter the workforce, the more it provides hope and belief that in the longer term, and in spite of obvious structural barriers and the micro-politics of the childcare workplace, graduate practitioners with their knowledge, pedagogical skills and critical thinking have the potential to develop a democratic form of professionalism.

My own recent research (Oates 2011) and that of others – for example, Simpson (2010) – show that early childhood studies graduates do emerge with critical thinking skills, providing them with insight into their own oppression. Unfortunately, in the present climate, this can mean experienced graduates moving out of the sector into more established professional roles, or being subject to a lack of equity with teachers working in other parts of the school curriculum. However, the ground is slowly shifting, and here in the UK, and in other parts of the world, there is strengthening recognition of the importance and value of early childhood pedagogy, underpinned by research. This is, in part, due to the growth and popularity over the last decade and more of specialist degrees such as BA (Hons) Early Childhood Studies. However, it is important that we, as practitioners and academics, remain vigilant for the sake of the youngest members of our society to ensure children's experiences of early childhood education and care are central to practice and policies, and are the best they can be. As Mac Naughton (2005) suggests, through critical thinking, practitioners must question the regimes of truth and analyse micro-practices of power in the workplace. Mac Naughton *et al.* (2003) also suggest that it is imperative early childhood practitioners bring critical activism into their work by being prepared to contest, reflect on and explore different truths about childhood.

In conclusion, Table 7.1 suggests ways in which early childhood studies graduates may use their knowledge and learning to move forward individually, collectively and to remain critically active and well read.

Table 7.1 Moving forward as an early childhood studies graduate and critical activist

Possible ways forward	Some options and ideas
Continue personal and professional development planning utilising all resources available to you.	Use the resources of your university's Career Development Centre before and after graduation, including job-seeking skills, interview skills and CV updating. What is your unique selling point (USP)?
Maintain and develop your critical, reflective, thinking skills and knowledge base.	Find ways to continue to reflect upon your practice, values and attitudes. Encourage others to do so in a supportive and collegiate manner.
Maintain academic and professional development through further training and development.	Look for opportunities in and outside the workplace. Consider postgraduate study, such as a master's degree specialising in early childhood.
Develop and enhance your understanding of practice and early years' pedagogy in a range of settings.	Widen your employment experience and be prepared to look at opportunities you might initially think are not for you. Undertake volunteering in your community. Take opportunities to work, travel and study abroad to widen your knowledge and understanding.
Find opportunities to work collectively and collaboratively with others to support the development of democratic professionalism.	Find ways of developing a community of practice. Join local forums and groups. Take mentoring and leadership opportunities to support new and less experienced colleagues. Support and input into training and development events with others.
Provide a voice for early childhood practitioners through engagement with external forums.	Support trade union and professional organizations by playing an active role. Join virtual and actual forums, consultations, groups and initiatives. Let your voice be heard, and in particular, take part in government consultations.
	Find opportunities to write and undertake research, perhaps with the support of your university tutors. Offer to come back and talk to current students to share your experiences.
Continue to read widely and keep up to date with local, national and international developments, research, policies and practice.	Join groups such as the European Early Childhood Education Research Association, attend conferences, read journals, engage in forums with others. Keep aware of local and regional changes and opportunities they may bring for you.

(Continued)

Table 7.1 (Continued)

Enhance your employability.	Many of the foregoing suggestions will enhance your employability. It is really important you gather information about opportunities in the sector. Early Childhood Studies degrees are a platform to many professional careers that include working with young children and families, many including postgraduate training. This includes family and community work, social work, nursing and midwifery, occupational therapy, public health, local government, psychological therapies, teaching in the early years, infant and junior, working and volunteering abroad at international schools, worldwide charities, the British Council and so on. Gather information and know what opportunities are available to you, utilising specialist university careers advisors and tutors. Look at opportunities on job websites, including local government, National Health Service and so on.

References and further reading

Abbott, L. & Pugh, G. (1998) *Training to Work in the Early Years*. Buckingham: Open University Press.

Allen, C. (2003) Desperately Seeking Fusion: On 'Joined Up Thinking', 'Holistic Practice' and the New Economy of Welfare Professional Power. *British Journal of Sociology* 54 (2): 287–306.

Bates, I. (1990) No Bleeding, Whining Minnies: The Role of the YTS in Class and Gender Reproduction. *British Journal of Education and Work* 2: 91–110.

Bates, I. (1991) Closely Observed Training: An Explanation of Links between Social Structures, Training and Identity. *International Studies in Sociology of Education* 1: 225–243. http://dx.doi.org.10.1080.0962021910010113 (accessed 23 April 2011).

Bates, I. (1994) A Job Which Is 'Right for Me'? Social Class, Gender and Individualization, in I. Bates & G. Riseborough (Eds), *Youth and Inequality*, pp. 14–31. Buckingham: Open University Press.

Bertram, T. & Pascal, C. (1995) Questions of Quality, in P. Gammage & J. Meighan (Eds), *Early Childhood Education: The Way Forward* (pp. 53–74). Derby: Education Now Books.

Boddy, J., Cameron, D., Moss, P., Mooney, A., Petri, P. & Statham, J. (2005) *Introducing Pedagogy into the Children's Workforce*. London: Thomas Coram Research Unit.

Bottero, W. (1992) The Changing Face of Professions: Gender and Explanations of Women's Entry into Pharmacy. *Work, Employment and Society* 6: 329–345.

Bourdieu, P. (1986) The Forms of Capital, in J. Richardson (Ed), *Handbook of Theory and Research for the Sociology of Education* (pp. 241–258). New York: Greenwood.

Brannen, J. & Moss, P (Eds) (2003) *Rethinking Children's Care*. Buckingham: Open University Press.

Brownhill, S. (2011) *The 'Brave' Man in the Early Years (0–8): The Ambiguities of Being a Role Model*. Unpublished doctoral thesis, University of Derby, UK.

Calder, P. (2006, 23 February) The Early Childhood Studies Network Response to the TDA consultation on QTS Standards. *Early Childhood Studies Degree Network*. www.uel.ac.uk/ecsdegreesnetwork/ (accessed 14 January 2014).

Cameron, C. (2006) Men in the Nursery Revisited: Issues of Male Workers and Professionalism. *Contemporary Issues in Early Childhood* 7 (1): 68–79. http://dx.doi.10.2304/ciec.2006.7.1.68 (accessed 2 January 2014).

Cameron, C., Owen, C. & Moss, P. (2001) *Entry, Retention and Loss: A Study of Childcare Students and Workers*. London: Thomas Coram Research Unit, Institute of Education, University of London.

Carlson, H.L. & Karp, J.M. (1997) Integration in Early Childhood: A Program in Three Countries. *International Journal of Early Years' Education* 5 (2): 107–117.

Children's Workforce Development Council (2008[1]) *Guidance to the Standards for the Award of Early Years Professional Status.* Leeds: CWDC.

Cleave, S. & Brown, S. (1991) *Early to School.* Windsor: NFER/Nelson.

Colley, H. (2006) Learning to Labour with Feeling: Class, Gender and Emotion in Childcare Education and Training. *Contemporary Issues in Early Childhood* 7 (1): 15–29. http://dx.doi.10.2304/ciec.2006.7.15 (accessed 2 January 2014).

Colley, H., James, D., Tedder, M. & Diment, K. (2003) Learning as Becoming in Vocational Education and Training: Class, Gender and the Role of Vocational Habitus. *Journal of Vocational Education and Training* 55 (1): 471–498. http://dx.doi.org/10.1080/13636820300200240 (accessed 2 July 2010).

Cooke, C. & Lawton, K. (2008) *For Love or Money: Pay, Progression and Professionalization in the 'Early Years' Workforce.* London: Institute for Public Policy Research.

Crompton, R. (1987) Gender, Status and Professionalism. *Sociology* 21: 413–428.

Dalli, C. (2010) Towards the Re-emergence of a Critical Ecology of the Early Childhood Profession in New Zealand. *Contemporary Issues in Early Childhood* 11 (1): 61–74. http://dx.doi.org/10.2304/ciec.2010.11.1.61 (accessed 14 January 2014).

Davies, C. (1996) The Sociology of Professions and the Profession of Gender. *Sociology* 30 (4): 661–678. http://soc.sagepub.com/cgi/content/abstract/30/4/661 (accessed 23 July 2013).

Department for Education (DfE) (2012) *Foundations for Quality: The Independent Review of Early Education and Childcare Qualifications. Final Report.* www.education.gov.uk/publications/standard/EarlyYearseducationandchildcare/Page1/DFE-0006802012 (accessed 16 April 2013).

Department for Education (DfE) (2013) *More Great Childcare: Raising Quality and Giving Parents More Choice.* www.education.gov.uk/publications/standard/publicationDetail/Page1/DFE-00002–2013 (accessed 16 April 2013).

Department for Education & Employment (DfEE) (1998) *Meeting the Childcare Challenge.* London: HMSO.

Department for Education & Skills (DfES) (2003) *Every Child Matters: Summary.* Nottingham: DfES. Ref. DfES/0672.

Department for Education & Skills (DfES) (2005) *Children's Workforce Strategy Consultation.* www.dfes.gov.uk/consultations.conResults.cfm?consultation (accessed 1 March 2006).

Department for Education & Skills (DfES) (2006a) *Children's Workforce Strategy: Building a World-Class Workforce for Children, Young People and Families. The Government's Response to the Consultation.* Nottingham: DfES.

Department for Education & Skills (DfES: 2006b) *Children's Workforce Strategy: Building an Integrated Qualifications Framework.* Nottingham: DfES.

Department for Education & Skills (DfES) (2007) *Children's Workforce Strategy Update Spring.* www.everychildmatters.gov.uk/resources-and-practice/IG00210/ (accessed 12 September 2008).

Dreyfus, H.L. & Rabinow, P. (1982) *Michel Foucault: Beyond Structuralism and Hermeneutics.* London: Harvester Wheatsheaf.

Evetts, J. (2003) The Sociological Analysis of Professionalism: Occupational Change in the Modern World. *International Sociology* 18 (2): 395–415.

Evetts, J. (2006) Introduction: Trust and Professionalism: Challenges and Occupational Changes. *Current Sociology* 54: 515–531.

Exworthy, M. & Halford, S. (Eds) (1999) *Professionalism and the New Managerialism in the Public Sector.* Buckingham: Open University Press.

Foucault, M. (1977) *Discipline and Power: The Birth of the Prison.* Harmondsworth: Penguin Books.

Gleeson, D. & Knights, D. (2006) Challenging Dualism: Public Professionalism in 'Troubled Times'. *Sociology* 40 (2): 277–295.

Hadfield, M. & Jopling, M. (2012) *Second National Survey of Practitioners with Early Years Professional Status.* Department for Education Research Report DFE-RR239a. Wolverhampton: University of Wolverhampton.

Haug, M. (1988) A Re-examination of the Hypothesis of Physician Deprofessionalisation. *Millbank Quarterly* 66 (Suppl. 2): 48–56.

Hendrick, H. (1994) *Child Welfare, England 1872–1989*. London: Routledge.

Hendrick, H. (1997) Constructions and Reconstructions of British Childhood, in A. James & A. Prout (Eds), *Constructing and Reconstructing Childhood: Contemporary Issues in the Sociological Study of Childhood*. 2nd ed. London: Falmer.

Independent (2013) Nick Clegg Blocks Nursery Shake-Up – and Says It Could Have Pushed Up Costs for Parents. www.independent.co.uk/life-style/health-and-families/health-news/nick-clegg-blocks-nursery-shakeup-and-says-it-could-have-pushed-up-costs-for-parents-8646502.html (accessed 27 June 2013).

James, A. & Prout, A. (Eds) (1997) *Constructing and Reconstructing Childhood: Contemporary Issues in the Sociological Study of Childhood*. 2nd ed. London: Falmer.

Laming, H. (2003) *The Victoria Climbie Inquiry*. London: Stationery Office D15.

Lewis, J. (2003) Developing Early Years Childcare in England, 1997–2002: The Choices for (Working) Mothers. *Social Policy & Administration* 37 (3): 219–238.

Mac Naughton, G. (2003) *Shaping Early Childhood: Learners, Curriculum and Context*. Maidenhead: Open University Press.

Mac Naughton, G. (2005) *Doing Foucault in Early Childhood Studies*. London: Routledge Falmer Press.

Manning-Morton, J. (2006) The Personal Is Professional: Professionalism and the Birth to Threes Practitioners. *Contemporary Issues in Early Childhood* 7 (1): 42–52. http://dx.doi.org/10.2304/ciec.2006.7.1.42 (accessed 14 January 2014).

Mansell, M. (1993) Primary Care. *Managing Schools Today* 2 (4): 22–23.

Mayall, B. (2002) *Towards a Sociology of Childhood: Thinking from Children's Lives*. Buckingham: Open University Press.

Miller, L. & Cable, C. (2012) *Professionalism in the Early Years*. London: Hodder Education.

Moriarty, V. (2000) Early Years Educators in Finland and England: Issues of Professionality. *International Journal of Early Years Education* 8 (3): 235–242.

Moss, P. (2003) *Beyond Caring: The Case for Reforming the Childcare and Early Years' Workforce*. London: Daycare Trust, The National Childcare Campaign.

Moss, P. (2006) Structures, Understandings and Discourses: Possibilities for Re-envisioning the Early Childhood Workers. *Contemporary Issues in the Early Years* 7 (1): 30–41. http://dx.do1.10.2304/ciec.2006.7.1.30 (accessed 7 May 2007).

Moss, P. & Petrie, P. (2002) *From Children's Services to Children's Spaces: Public Policy, Children and Childhood*. London: Routledge Falmer.

Moyles, J. (2001) Passion, Paradox and Professionalism in Early Years Education. *Early Years* 21 (2): 81–95.

Mumsnet (2013) *Changes to Nursery and Childminder Staff Ratios*. www.mumsnet.com/jobs/changes-to-nursery-staff-ratios (accessed 27 June 2013).

NCB (1992) *The Future of Training in the Early Years: A Discussion Paper*. London: Early Childhood Unit, National Children's Bureau.

Neuman, M. (2005) 'Governance of early childhood systems: recent developments in OECDE countries', *Early Years* 25 (2): 129–142.

Nutbrown, C. (2013) *Shaking the Foundations of Quality? Why 'Childcare' Policy Must Not Lead to Poor-Quality Early Education and Care*. Sheffield: University of Sheffield.

Oakley, A. (Ed) (2005) *The Ann Oakley Reader: Gender, Women and Social Science*. Bristol: Policy Press.

Oates, R.A. (2011) *Constructing the Early Childhood Professional: A Research Project Capturing the Voice of Early Childhood Practitioners, Their Experiences of the Workplace during a Period of Professionalization, and the Impact of Higher Education*. Unpublished doctoral thesis, University of Derby, UK.

Oberheumer, P. (2012) Who Is an Early Years Professional? Reflections on Policy Diversity in Europe, in L. Miller & C. Cable (Eds), *Professionalism in the Early Years* (pp. 131–141). Abingdon: Hodder Education.

Organisation for Economic Co-operation and Development (OECD) (2001) Starting Strong. Early Childhood Education and Care. Paris: OECD.

Organisation for Economic Co-operation and Development (OECD) (2006) Starting Strong II. Early Childhood Education and Care. Paris: OECD.

Osgood, J. (2006a) Deconstructing Professionalism in the Early Years: Resisting the Regulatory Gaze. *Contemporary Issues in Early Childhood* 7 (1): 5–14.

Osgood, J. (2006b) Editorial: Rethinking 'Professionalism' in the Early Years: Resisting the Regulatory Gaze. *Contemporary Issues in Early Childhood* 7 (1): 1–4. http://dx.doi.10.2304/ciec2006.7.1.5 (accessed 15 May 2007).

Osgood, J. (2009) Childcare Workforce Reform in England and 'the Early Years Professional': A Critical Discourse Analysis. *Journal of Education Policy* 24 (6): 733–751. http://dx.doi.org/10.1080/02680930903244557 (accessed 21 March 2011).

Ozga, J. (1995) Deskilling a Profession: Professionalism, Deprofessionalisation and the New Managerialism, in H. Bush & R. Saran (Eds), *Managing Teachers as Professionals in Schools* (pp. 21–38). London: Kogan Page.

Ozga, J. (2000) *Policy Research in Educational Settings: Contested Terrain.* Buckingham: Open University Press.

Penn, H. (2007) Childcare Market and Managements: How the United Kingdom Government Has Reshaped Its Role in Developing Early Childhood Education and Care. *Contemporary Issues in Early Childhood* 8 (3): 192–207.

Penn, H. (2011) *Quality in Early Childhood Services: An International Perspective.* Maidenhead: Open University Press / McGraw-Hill Education.

Pugh, G. (Ed) (2001) *Contemporary Issues in the Early Years.* 3rd ed. London: Paul Chapman.

Pugh, G. & Duffy, B. (Eds) (2006) *Contemporary Issues in the Early Years.* 4th ed. London: SAGE.

Qvortrup, J. (1991) *Childhood as a Social Phenomenon – An Introduction to a Series of National Reports.* Eurosocial Report 36/1991. Vienna: European Centre.

Randall, V. (2000) *The Politics of Child Daycare in Britain.* Oxford: Oxford University Press.

Reay, D. (2000) A Useful Extension of Bourdieu's Conceptual Framework?: Emotional Capital as a Way of Understanding Mothers' Involvement in Their Children's Education. *Sociological Review* 48 (4): 568–585.

Robins, V. & Silcock, P. (2001) The Invisible Professionals: English School Nursery Nurses Talk about Their Jobs. *European Early Childhood Education Research Journal* 9 (1): 23–40.

Rose, N. (1999) *Powers of Freedom: Reframing Political Thought.* Cambridge: Cambridge University Press.

Simpson, D. (2010) Becoming Professional? Exploring Early Years Professional Status and Its Implications for Workforce Reform in England. *Journal of Early Childhood Research* 8 (3): 269–281. http://ecr.sagepub.com/content/8/3/269 (accessed 23 March 2011).

Skeggs, B. (1988) Gender Reproduction and Further Education: Domestic Apprenticeships. *British Journal of Sociology of Education* 9: 131–149.

Skeggs, B. (1997) *Formations of Class and Gender.* London: SAGE.

Skeggs, B. (2003) *Class, Self, Culture.* London: Routledge.

Sylva, K., Melhuish, E., Sammons, P., Siraj-Blatchford I. and Taggart, B. (2004) *The Effective Provision of Pre-School Education (EPPE) Project: Final Report: A Longitudinal Study Funded by the DfES 1997–2004.* Nottingham: DfES.

Witz, A. (1992) *Professions and Patriarchy.* London: Routledge.

Wood, E. (Ed) (2008) *The Routledge Reader in Early Childhood Education.* London: Routledge.

Chapter 8

The student practitioner as future leader

Ellen Yates and Helen Simmons

In this chapter we will:

- Consider the role of leadership in early childhood and what the role entails.
- Identify skills and characteristics that may support leadership.
- Consider what makes an effective team and the pressures and constraints that can impact upon effective teamwork.
- Consider the role of effective communication and reflection within teamwork.

Introduction

Leadership in early childhood is not easy to define due to the relational nature of working with young children, the diversity of settings providing for their care and education, and the wide range of roles and responsibilities which are implicit within these settings. Roles and responsibilities inevitably overlap, and a 'leader' in an early years' setting may not be easy to distinguish from any other member of staff. However, strong and effective leadership is essential to the smooth running of early years' settings, and research identifies strong links between effective leadership and 'quality' practice (Siraj-Blatchford & Manni 2008). Identifying what is involved in leadership is therefore of paramount importance. This chapter will consider what is involved in a leadership role in practice and its importance in ensuring effective teamwork to provide the very best practice we can offer the children in our care.

Leadership and management – what is the difference?

Leadership is often confused with management, and the two roles often overlap; however, there are some specific differences between the two roles, and it is helpful to make clear distinctions between them.

Activity

Using your own experiences of work settings consider the terms *leadership* and *management*. Write down as many words that you can think of that relate to each.

In the previous activity you may have identified some differences in relation to hierarchy and status, and specific responsibilities. Managers tend to have responsibility for administration, budgets and the organization, 'hiring and firing' of staff, and are often (but not always) physically removed from the day-to-day running of settings (in offices). Managers also often take a 'top-down' approach to decision making, based on factors that are not necessarily driven by 'quality practice' as defined by staff but rather based on financial or business-related factors, or in some cases, factors that are not even communicated to staff. It has been suggested that management roles encompass 'male' characteristics, such as aggression, competition, hierarchy and individualism, where decision making is 'present-oriented' rather than 'future-oriented' (Blackmore cited in Aubrey 2011). We need, however, to move away from gender stereotypes and recognise that these characteristics are not exclusive to men. For example, a number of private companies run chains of early years' settings for profit and are managed by both sexes; in a profit-making scenario, managers of either sex may adopt these characteristics within their role. It is also important to recognise that many 'managers' are also 'leaders' and may have responsibility for both the 'business' side of settings and also the 'practice' side, so there may not be a clear distinction between these roles in some settings.

Leaders are usually directly involved with staff, children and families, and have some influence over the practice that occurs in the setting. Leaders provide direction or vision, based upon their philosophy or beliefs about 'quality' practice and what this means for children and families. Of course this is also influenced by experience, qualifications and knowledge of children and families. According to Horner (2003 cited in Moyles 2006:3),

> Leadership is less a specific set of behaviours than it is creating an environment in which people are motivated to produce and move in the direction of the leader.

Horner's view suggests 'followers' are 'motivated' and willing to follow the leader's direction; this in turn implies an understanding or at least acceptance of the overall 'vision' of the leader. If this 'vision' is not shared or accepted by staff then this is likely to lead to conflict and ineffective practice; this will be discussed later in the chapter. In the sense of 'leading practice' a leader may be a 'change agent' who is responsible for ensuring the best-quality practice and influencing others employed in the setting.

The early years sector is still predominately female, and some have suggested that the gendered nature of the profession influences the leadership styles and strategies adopted. Shakeshaft's research (cited in Aubrey 2011) on women's leadership identified the following principles and may resonate with many working in early childhood presently.

- Collaboration
- Power sharing
- Caring
- Relationships
- Shared decision making.

Shakeshaft's work suggests that women work differently in teams in relation to men and are motivated by different concerns. Though we may recognise some of these differences, Whalley (cited in Miller *et al.* 2012) highlights the dangers of stereotyping and points to Rodd's research (2006) which suggests that styles of leadership may be influenced more by the situation rather than gender.

Leadership roles within early childhood

Whalley (cited in Miller *et al.* 2012) identifies how the changing landscape of the early years sector has also produced confusion around leadership roles, and this looks to be further complicated by the new Early Years Teacher role, which is currently (at time of writing) being introduced. Integrated children's centres provide a wide range of services and involve a number of different professionals working together. Due to the complex and diverse nature of integrated children's centres, the Integrated Centre Leader (ICL) will inevitably be involved in aspects of 'management' as well as 'leadership'. The Early Years Professional (EYP) role, however, was designed specifically to lead practice and envisioned as a 'change agent'. However, as Whalley identifies, due to the diversity of settings where EYPs are employed, the role of the EYP is still ambiguous (cited in Miller *et al.* 2012). The new Early Years Teacher (EYT) role looks to further confuse matters, as this could devalue the role of the EYP and ICL. What remains to be seen is how this role will be distinguished in terms of equality of income, as this ultimately will determine how each of these roles are valued by the current government. Interestingly, the new Early Years Teacher role (which qualifies the recipient to work with children aged 0–5) will not be equivalent to Qualified Teacher Status (which qualifies recipients to work with children 3–11). This appears to perpetuate the lack of value placed upon the early years sector generally and may lead to confusion in relation to pay scales, especially for those working with children aged 3–5, as those with QTS will be paid on one scale while EYTs will be paid on another, while both doing the same job.

It can be seen that leadership roles vary according to the setting, and there is no 'specific recipe' for leadership roles in the current climate; however, there are some general principles and a burgeoning research culture within the area at present. The next section will look at some specific theories in relation to leadership.

Theories about leadership

Many theories about leadership have been derived from leadership in the business sector, and historically there has been less research in early childhood; however, this is changing and there are now a number of studies available, and these are increasing

(Mujis *et al.* 2004; Moyles 2006; Siraj-Blatchford & Manni 2008; Aubrey 2011; Rodd 2004). According to Handy (cited in Aubrey 2011), there are four main types of theory in relation to leadership; these are as follows:

- Traits theories – personal traits and characteristics.
- Style theories – autocratic/democratic/charismatic.
- Contingency theories – situational – task, group, position of leader.
- 'Best fit' approaches – leader, followers, task, environment.

Traits theories focus upon the traits or characteristics of the leader and suggest that one needs specific qualities in order to fulfil this role. Style theories are based upon the 'style' that the leader adopts in order to engender action in the team or group. Contingency and 'best-fit' theories pay more attention to the context and the need for flexibility to deal with continual change. We will look at each of these in turn.

Leadership qualities and traits

Some have suggested that leaders require specific qualities or characteristics in order to be successful. The research of Mujis *et al.* (2004) and Moyles (2006) identifies some key skills and personal qualities as being important for leadership. These include: vision, patience and warmth, supporting, empowering and enabling staff, good communication skills, responding to parents and setting the culture. Aubrey (2011:30) identifies four categories of leaders based on personal characteristic variables: *'leaders as guides'*, *'leaders as strategists'*, *leaders as motivators'* and *'leaders as entrepreneurial and business-oriented'*. Within her research participants identified a number of specific qualities of effective leaders. These include the following:

- 'Holistic' values, caring and understanding.
- Vision, direction, strategy, decision maker, problem solver, creative.
- Role model, guide, sets standards.
- Listens, gives advice, is approachable, a motivator, generates staff development.
- Up-to-date, changes with policy.
- Influence on staff and community.

(Aubrey 2011:41)

Though there are slight variations there is general agreement that some qualities and certainly key skills are important. A recent small-scale research project carried out by the authors (Yates & Simmons 2012) concurs with these ideas and identified that qualities in leaders are valued differently, depending on experience and length of time in the profession, which supports the previous findings of Aubrey (2011). Participants with less than five years' experience in the authors' study identified 'empathy' and 'listening skills' as important qualities for leaders, but more experienced participants (five or more years' experience) placed more value on 'vision' and knowledge of current policy. This suggests that as practitioners progress in their careers, they value different types of leadership. Effective communication has been identified as a key skill for leaders in most of the studies discussed, and it seems unlikely that any team could function well without this. It could be argued, however, that many of these qualities and skills are not specific to 'leaders' and could be seen as important for all who work with young children.

Leadership styles

As discussed earlier, it could be argued that an effective leader demands specific personality types or certain characteristics; however, some suggest that the style of leadership that is adopted is more important than the qualities of the leader. Neuge-bauer (cited in Stacey 2009:31) identifies a range of different leadership styles which, when seen on a continuum, may be appropriate at specific times and in certain contexts as follows:

- Taskmaster – authoritarian, task-oriented

The taskmaster is focussed primarily on the task at hand and will ensure that the task is completed irrespective of relationships or complications. For this reason the taskmaster may adopt an authoritarian approach which ensures that his or her authority is not challenged.

- Comrade – relationships before task

The comrade is much more interested in developing harmonious relationships in the team and deems this the most important area. The comrade ensures that the individual in the team is supported and listened to, and encourages the team to be involved in decision making. However, this may mean that the task is secondary and relationships may complicate decision making.

- Unleader – laissez-faire, chance

The unleader is much more relaxed about his or her leadership style and often leaves decision making to individuals and allows each person within the team to be independent. While this may lead to the use of initiative, it also leaves the task to chance, and the unleader does not provide focus or vision for the team.

- Motivator – relationships and task

The motivator can be seen as a mixture of all of the styles as this type of leader focuses on both relationships and the task, and also provides an overall vision for the team. This leader ensures that individuals are motivated to achieve the task, usually by utilising each individual's strengths and interests. The team is empowered to use initiative but also provided with some focus on the task at hand.

It is clear to see that a leader may adopt all or some of these styles at different times, and though these may be helpful to describe behaviour, they do not neces-sarily pay attention to the influence of an ever-changing context.

Other styles of leadership include the following:

- Directing – Specific, clear guidelines.
- Coaching – Advises, gives praise.
- Supporting – Less supervision, staff involved in making decisions.
- Delegating – Freedom to organize own work, staff take decisions on their own.

Rodd (2004) suggested that one of the key issues in the overall effectiveness of a team is with the leadership style adopted by the designated leader. The role of this person and the way in which he or she managed a wide range of responsibilities were regarded by the participants of her study as having a major impact on the overall development of the team within the early childhood centre. Rodd's research gives an important insight into the way early childhood teams view teamwork from both a staff member and leader perspective:

> These data indicate that many early childhood professionals understand that teamwork is more than just turning up for work each day. It involves a special conceptualisation of the roles and responsibilities of both the leader and each team member. For leaders, teamwork means acting more as a facilitator than a superior. For staff members, it means taking an active role in the work situation rather than being a passive follower of instructions and directions.
>
> (Rodd 2004:103)

These theories, while helpful, place most of the emphasis on the leader and suggest that our personalities are fixed. The following theories take into account how context can influence and change our behaviour, thus placing more emphasis on a wider range of factors than the leader.

Contextual theories

Contextual theories focus less on the qualities of the leader and more on the context within which the leader works, which includes the environment, others involved and influencing factors such as the culture of the organization and social factors. The International Leadership Project (Hujala & Puroila cited in Aubrey 2011) sees leadership as

- Situational
- Socially constructed
- Interpretative.

Therefore leadership has to be considered in relation to the social interaction in the setting, the community and the social and cultural context. These ideas are based on Bronfenbrenner's ecological theory, which identifies the myriad of influential factors which impact upon practice in any setting (see Hujala & Puroila cited in Aubrey 2011). This suggests that it is difficult to provide a 'prescription' for leadership roles, due to numerous differing variables involved and the unique nature of each setting. The distributed leadership model (Waniganayake cited in Aubrey 2011) proposes similar ideas, but identifies some key principles, as follows:

- Organizational learning at centre
- Joint/multiple leaders with expertise
- Participatory/decentralised approach
- Building relationships through existing knowledge
- Empowerment based on competence
- Culture of learning/ shared knowledge.

This distributed model is one that may be most familiar to practitioners in early years' settings as it takes account of the multiple and overlapping roles within the sector. Certainly parallels can be seen in integrated children's centres, where there are a range of professionals with expertise in different fields working together with a participatory approach. In these types of settings there will not necessarily be one 'leader' as such, but rather a core team of professionals who may share roles and responsibilities.

In their Effective Leadership in the Early Years Sector study (ELEYS 2007) Siraj-Blatchford and Manni found three key variables in effective settings, contextual literacy, collaboration and improvement of children's learning outcomes (Siraj-Blatchford & Manni cited in Miller *et al.* 2012).

This suggests that the contextual literacy of leaders and the core team and the ability to be flexible in the face of changing circumstances are more important that adopting a fixed 'style' of leadership, or possession of specific personal qualities. Their findings also suggest that collaboration is fundamental to effective teamwork, which further supports Waniganayake's distributed model of shared leadership.

Southworth (cited in Stacey 2009) proposed the notion of 'situational leadership', which concurs with the previous models and identifies the following:

- *Contextual literacy* – leader reads situation and people within it
- Understanding of settings as *dynamic organisms*
- Flexibility to deal with *new energies, ideas and conflicts.*

This model seems to take into account the continual change inherent in the early childhood sector as well as the recognition that personalities and 'styles' of leadership also change according to context. This model can also be applied to shared leadership and recognises the need for continual review and the need for flexibility rather than a 'fixed' approach or 'style'. Reflective practice then is embedded within this model and will be fundamental to the development of a 'learning culture'. Whalley (2011) also recognises the need for a leader to be creative and a 'possibility thinker', one who can see many solutions to problems and has a 'can do' approach to overcoming challenges.

Activity
- Consider an effective leader you know or have worked with.
- Can you identify any of the foregoing theories or ideas?

To conclude this section, it is difficult to provide a 'recipe' for an effective leader, but we can extract some important factors from the views discussed which may be important for a leader.

An effective leader needs to be:

- an excellent communicator
- flexible and tolerant
- creative, able to see challenges positively
- able to adopt different 'styles' of leadership according to the context
- empathetic and contextually literate
- motivated by a strong vision and clear philosophy of practice.

> Good leaders are generally thought to be people who are able to think and act creatively in routine and non-routine situations and who set out to influence the actions, beliefs and feelings of others.
>
> (Doyle & Smith cited in Whalley 2011:17)

Effective communication

Research has demonstrated time and again the central role of effective communication in leadership and effective practice (Siraj-Blatchford & Manni 2008; Rodd 2004; Yates and Simmons 2012). As Hey and Oates discuss in Chapter Five, working in the early childhood sector is a relational activity involving a diverse range of people; it follows that clear and confident communication is imperative. This is not always straightforward, however, and self-awareness and a clear insight into how we communicate can be helpful in developing effective and positive strategies.

Whatever role you play in a team it is important to know yourself; working in a multi-professional, diverse team requires flexibility and tolerance.

> In order to build effective and trusting relationships we need to understand ourselves and have the confidence to share more with others. This process of cultural change is essential if we are to provide better services for children.
>
> (DfES cited in Stacey 2009)

It is important for all members of the team, especially the leader, to reflect upon how they communicate. In a leadership role clear and assertive communication is vital for a number of reasons: to ensure that all members of the team have a clear understanding of their roles and responsibilities within the setting, and to ensure that all members of the team are listened to and respected, and have the opportunity to make decisions regarding their own practice. Manni and Siraj-Blatchford (2008:15) identified 'transparency in regard to expectations, practices and processes' within the effective settings in their study, therefore communicating that a strong shared philosophy and 'shared understandings' (Manni & Siraj-Blatchford 2007:13) are essential in providing a unified approach to practice (this should, however, leave room for individuality and difference). How the leader communicates with her team then is key, as Stacey (2009:43) identifies:

> Your personal behaviour can influence the way ideas are taken up, and communicating effectively with others can bring about change.

Clear and assertive communication involves the following:

- Understanding yourself and how others respond to you
- Listening as much as talking
- Respecting others views and opinions.

How do you communicate? Consider the following. Can you identify with any of these approaches?

- Passive – avoidance, accepting status quo. Do you lack the confidence to challenge the views of others, especially when you do not agree with them? Are you quiet in meetings? Do you avoid conflict rather than dealing with issues?
- Aggressive – manipulative, coercive, dominating. If you want to get your point across, do you rely on speaking more loudly than others, or ignoring others' views? Think about your body language – how do others respond to you? Do you dominate in meetings?
- Assertive – open and honest communication, room for difference, discussion and resolution. Are you able to resolve conflicting viewpoints? Can you 'agree to differ'? Are you able to discuss difficult issues and challenge differences of opinion confidently?

In the previous task you may have identified that there are areas for improvement in the way you communicate with others; awareness of this is the first step to considering ways to improve your approach. It may be helpful to practice different ways to contribute to discussions, bearing in mind the factors discussed. You may need to practice listening and responding positively to others' viewpoints, or you may need to practice contributing to discussions more effectively. Consider how to deal with conflicting viewpoints. Can a compromise be reached? Setting yourself targets may help you to improve your skills over time.

According to Stacey (2009) there are a number of factors the leader may need to consider in communicating effectively:

- Why: What is the purpose or objective of your communication? Is action expected and if so by whom? How will you ensure that action takes place?
- Who: Do you need to communicate with specific individuals or the whole team? What language will you use? Can you use professional language or will you need

to modify your language to ensure everyone understands (If your audience is a parent or carer, for example)?

- What: Does your audience need to know? Do you need to explain everything (such as reasons for your actions)? Do they need all the details?
- Where: The context will be important, depending on the type of communication. Is it a meeting involving a group or does it involve one individual? Confidentiality will need to be considered here; you may not want to be overheard.
- When: Ensure you allow enough time to discuss issues thoroughly and allow time for listening and resolution if this is necessary. The time of day/week is also important to consider.
- How: Self-awareness is important here – for example, your tone of voice and your body language. You may need to prepare carefully, particularly if you are discussing sensitive issues.

Team building

> Effective leadership and collective responsibility – that is, teamwork – can have a major impact on the quality of the service offered.
>
> (Rodd cited in Miller *et al.* 2012:264)

In the earlier discussions some of the elements of effective teamwork have become apparent. Recent authors have identified that a shared common goal or vision is fundamental to any team (Rodd 2006; Stacey 2009); others have identified key aspects of shared practice, such as 'sustained shared thinking' (Siraj-Blatchford & Manni 2008). Here we will consider what else is important in building an effective team, firstly by considering what 'teams' are.

Consider your own experiences of being a member of a team and being a member of a group. How do these differ? Use the following examples to help you.

    A football team
    An orchestra
    A yoga group
    A restaurant team

Do all of these examples have a common goal? What is required of the participants? What will make these teams effective?

In the foregoing examples you can identify some differences between 'groups' and 'teams' in terms of individual motivations for action. In teams, roles are interrelated and individual behaviour may impact upon others. For example, in the orchestra, each member will be doing different activities but will be interdependent in achieving the common goal (the piece of music); this involves each person playing his or her role expertly, and in collaboration with others. Individuals in the yoga group, however, may be working towards a common goal, but each individual's action is not dependent on others, and individual action will not impact upon others.

In early years' settings, roles are also interdependent to some degree, and though each member will be performing different roles, each will contribute towards the common goal of quality practice; like the orchestra, each member of the early years' team will need to be qualified and highly competent in his or her practice or field for the team to be effective.

Rodd (2006) identifies some key principles for effective teams.

- Pursuit of a common philosophy, ideals and values
- Commitment to working through issues
- Shared responsibility
- Open and honest communication
- Access to a support system.

In the previous activity you may have recognised some of these ideas and will certainly be able to apply them to an early years' setting. As discussed previously, a shared philosophy or common goal is important, but this needs to be flexible enough to cope with a diversity of views, professional approaches and personalities. For this reason it is important for members of a team to have a sense of belonging and to know that they are valued and respected, and to have some ownership of the principles that guide their practice. Opportunities to contribute to decision making is therefore important, and time needs to be made available for this to occur. Similarly, the role of critical reflection is vital to effective teamwork in order for members to learn from each other and work collaboratively to improve practice; this also needs time and space to occur effectively. Siraj-Blatchford and Manni (2008) identified the importance of *'encouraging reflection: which acts as an impetus for change and the motivation for ongoing learning and development'*.

Following on from Rodd's ideas, Adair (cited in NCSL 2003) identifies three main elements within effective teams:

- The task: This needs to be accomplished.
- The group: Relationships need to be nurtured and maintained.
- The individual: Each member has his or her own motivation, ways of working and needs.

The leader will be responsible for ensuring that each of these elements is attended to within the setting and will need to develop ways to achieve this.

Activity

In what ways can each of these aspects be monitored and developed by the leader? Fill in Table 8.1 with ideas from your own experience in early years' settings.

Table 8.1 Elements of an effective team

The task	The group	The individual

Belbin (2013) developed an approach to roles within teams, suggesting that effective teams need a range of people each with differing skills, interests and expertise. Belbin identified a number of specific 'team roles' as follows:

- Resource investigator: Sociable, liaises with others, brings people together.
- Coordinator: Keeps group focused, has overview of team goals.
- Shaper: Keeps on task, focuses group back to task.
- Completer/finisher: Good at detail and meeting deadlines.
- Implementer: Practical, organizer, puts plans into practice.
- Monitor/evaluator: Analyses, dependable, good at detail.
- Team worker: Supportive, uncompetitive, popular but in background.
- Plant: Creative, good ideas and suggestions, but not interested in detail.
- Specialist: An expert with in-depth knowledge of the key area.

(Belbin 2013)

Activity

- Do you identify with any of these roles personally?
- Can you identify any of these roles within your own settings or past experiences?
- Do you think these roles overlap?
- How helpful do you think 'role types' are in building a team?

Conflict

Conflict within teams in an inevitable part of your professional life; however, the way in which it is dealt with will determine whether it is a positive or negative experience. To try to avoid all conflict is unrealistic; it is a natural part of teamwork. Instead, conflict, when led well, can bring about creativity and new ideas; providing an environment where people within a team feel free to disagree with each other safely is a hugely valuable but not easily achieved part of effective teamwork.

> Team work is about trust, giving staff the opportunity to develop decision making skills. Good team players give their staff the facts and let them have a say in decisions that affect them.
>
> (Sadek & Sadek 2004:12)

Activity

Consider your own experiences:
Can you identify barriers to effective teamwork?
Identify aspects that have or may cause conflict.

Rather than viewing conflict as purely negative and something best avoided, leaders should view such situations as an *integral part of change management* (Smith & Langston 1999:165). Instead of seeing differences in opinion as possible threats, opportunities to change practice in a more positive way could be highly positive:

> When handled properly (conflict) can result in better ideas and approaches, clarification of individual views and renewed interest and creativity, often regarding long-standing problems that would otherwise remain beneath the surface.
>
> (Smith & Langston 1999:165)

It is part of the leader's role to negotiate the individual characters of the team to bring about positive change as a result of conflicting situations. Inevitably there will be individuals in teams who can on occasion be difficult to work with for a variety of reasons, and this may result in tensions. Leaders must strive to encourage individuals within teams to work to their own strengths and facilitate team members to bring about positive change in accordance with their individual needs and areas of expertise. This is a difficult skill to manage and one that may be achievable only through much experience and reflection, but it is a vital skill for effective leadership.

When conflict becomes a barrier to effective teamwork and begins to get in the way of the job that needs to be done, it is largely the leader's role to facilitate the situation to bring about a positive outcome. This may begin by exploring the reasons behind the conflict; research into conflicting teams within early years' settings has found some common root causes. Sadek and Sadek (2004) identify some common causes of conflict within teams:

- Policies
- Leadership style – supportive or bossy?
- Unwritten value systems
- Structure
- Administration – clear roles

- Limited staff time
- Disparity in qualifications
- Transitory staff
- Individual value systems – personal views and experiences
- Negative attitudes
- Unconventional holders of power
- Shift systems.

Research carried out by the authors (Yates & Simmons 2012) identified breakdown in communication as a common cause for conflict among teams. This was a theme that remained constant in responses to the research. It is important to acknowledge that personality traits are an important characteristic here; individuals will not all react in the same way to the foregoing. Smith and Langston (1999:167) describe this as a person's *'tolerance rating'*, whereby such situations may cause *'disturbances or minor protests amongst some people, where others would readily explode'*. While age, experience and individual differences all obviously play a part in the way people respond to potential conflicting situations, breakdowns in communication or feelings of not being consulted remain a common root cause of conflict.

When team members believe they are excluded from information or their views aren't listened to, this can lead to them feeling vulnerable and anxious; this commonly results in tension in teams. Within the current economic climate when jobs are not secure in some cases, this facilitates an environment in which conflict can occur. It is part of the leader's role to communicate effectively with the team and contain the anxieties that may be building due to the uncertain climate we currently live in.

Leading in a time of change

Few early childhood professionals have been unaffected by the current political, social and economic changes, bringing in its train cultural change to patterns in the workforce and family life. This has necessitated adaption to new ways of working by individual staff, team leaders and their organisations.

(Aubrey 2007:60)

Leadership within the current climate results in demands in terms of leadership style. In relation to the foregoing, change can result in anxiety, leading to potential conflicting situations; it is largely how this change is managed that will determine how smoothly the process goes through and ultimately how positively the change is viewed on both an individual and a team level.

What is change?

Stacey (2009:86) describes change as something that occurs every day for any *dynamic and living organism*. It does not need to be a stressful or anxiety-inducing situation as long as it is experienced with some stability and security. The process of change in terms of how it is communicated, facilitated and led makes a huge impact on how stressful the change is or how negatively it is viewed. Other common features of change include the following:

- It is inevitable
- Necessary
- A process
- Occurs in individuals, organizations and societies
- Can be anticipated and planned for
- Is a highly emotional process
- Can cause tension and stress
- Is resisted by many people
- Can be adjusted to by individuals and groups with the support of the leader
- Entails development growth in attitudes and skills, policies and procedures, and is best facilitated on the basis of diagnosed needs.

(Rodd 2004:128)

Types of change

Throughout your careers and indeed throughout your everyday life you will be involved in change; the type of change and the way it is led and received by those around you determine the impact of it. There are different types of change which you will come across. Rodd (cited in Whalley 2011:85) identified types of change as: *incremental, induced, routine, crisis, innovative and transformational*. For leaders the four types that require the most strategic consideration are the following.

1. Induced change: *This relates to a conscious decision that some aspect of practice relating to people or processes needs to be changed* (Whalley 2011:85) – for example, the review and redistribution of staff across the setting to allow for experiences to vary and development to progress.
2. Innovative change: *The leader seeks to introduce new practices in order to further the mission of a setting* (Whalley 2011:85) – for example, active participation and consideration of children's view on their outdoor learning environment.
3. Incremental change: *Through planning meetings or general day-to-day discussion* (Stacey 2009:87).
4. Transformational change: *This is where the organization is radically altered* (Stacey 2009:87).

Change from the individual perspective

As human beings we are creatures of habit; change is often something that results in feelings of insecurity, anxiety and resistance. It means we have to look at ourselves, the way we work individually and with others and our effectiveness. People often reflect on a change with positive feelings, but while the change is being introduced and during the process of change, there is often a very different dominating feeling! As mentioned previously, change can often result in feelings of stress from an individual perspective, resulting in conflict or at least tension among teams. The way in which change is dealt with may be determined by the sort of person you are and the way you manage change within your personal life.

Activity

- What are your recent experiences of change?
- What did you see as the role of others in helping you manage this change?

It is the leader's role to consider the impact of change from an individual's perspective. Regardless of specific change that is occurring, there are, according to Smith and Langston (1999), seven common characteristics that form the basis for an effective change programme:

1. Reciprocity: All parties should be able to give and take; understanding the problem from another angle helps diagnosis and increases transfer of information.
2. Openness: Both parties need to receive inputs from each other, including feedback and new ideas.
3. Realistic expectations: Both of others and yourself – try to counteract any impressions of enormous benefits by not overselling yourself or the project.
4. Expectations of reward: Some token of future reward is necessary as evidence of help and success – for example, more opportunities for staff for variety or responsibility.
5. Structure: It is important that roles and relationships are as clearly defined as working procedures.
6. Minimum threat: Disturbances rather than benefits are often seen as the outcome. Any change must actively seek to minimise such a perception.
7. Involvement of all parties: Everyone should be able to be involved, although the programme will inevitably make some demands of individuals at different stages.

(Smith & Langston 1999:74)

Defining quality

The Statutory Framework for The Early Years Foundation Stage stresses the importance of *improving quality and consistency and developing a universal standard* (EYFS 2007:7). Yet Moss and Pence suggest that quality childcare is, *to a large extent, in the eye of the beholder, and it is true that there are many criteria by which to judge quality* (Moss & Pence cited in Stacey 2009:2). This country has seen a move to improve the overall quality of provision for children and families over recent years, with reviews and revisions to existing legislation and frameworks (The Every Child Matters agenda [DfES 2003], Early Years Foundation Stage [DfES 2007], Families in the Foundation Years, Supporting Families in the Foundation Years [DfE, DfH 2011]). Much of this relates to a drive to encourage those who aim to or already work with children and families to work with and understand the role of other agencies and professionals, improve their professional knowledge and evaluate practice and provision (Miller *et al.* 2011).

Evaluating quality

Quality evaluation is a fundamental aspect of the world we live in. Through regular standardisation, reflection of practice and reviews of processes we are able to ensure performance levels do not drop from what is expected. Within an early years context, this includes assessing performance management from the perspective of not only educational attainments but also the satisfaction of those involved; it is a fundamental part of the leader's role to ensure that all perspectives are valued and listened to from a quality perspective.

Along with critical reflection as an important part of developing and maintaining quality within the early years, higher staff qualifications are also correlated with higher quality provision (Miller & Cable 2011). As previously mentioned within the chapter, early years practitioner qualifications are something that is constantly under review, along with the debate relating to what level a person working with very young children should aim for. Research also suggests that, along with the qualification a practitioner holds, in-service training is another important aspect of developing and maintaining childcare quality and improving outcomes for children. This does, however, depend on the quality of the training itself; research suggests it is valuable only if it is *of sufficient length and intensity* (Fukkink & Lont cited in Miller & Cable 2011:63). This requires commitment from leaders to provide opportunities for high-quality continuing professional development for members of staff.

Activity

Try to list the different methods of evaluating quality within an early years context.

What are your own experiences of these?

Another fundamental component in relation to promoting quality of provision is opportunities for discussion and reflection within teams. Through regular review meetings, peer observation opportunities and both informal and formal sharing of ideas it is possible to learn from mistakes, listen to the views of children, other professionals and parents and ultimately move forward with practice.

> Unless practitioners come together to discuss and share views, we weaken our position as advocates for children, unable to articulate our views on what children need or to challenge policy and practice that does not place the child at the centre.
>
> (Nutbrown cited in Stacey 2009:12)

Quality of leadership

The quality of provision is often associated with the quality of leadership. The work environment promoted through effective leadership along with active involvement in decision making (Whelan cited in Aubrey 2007) results in low staff turnover, which as a result raises social and emotional development in children (Hayden cited in Aubrey 2007). The ethos promoted within the environment of a setting through an effective leader is one of the key aspects of ensuring high-quality provision.

> Leaders play a central role in the creation of quality provision for young children and their families in the climate and culture of their organisation and hence, professional growth for staff. In order to discharge this function, leaders will need to have ongoing support for leader development.
>
> (Aubrey 2007:85)

Quality assurance

Leaders within early years' settings are ultimately accountable for quality. Another important aspect of their role is to ensure that *quality assurance measures are in place* (Moyles 2006:20). This means working with the necessary professional organizations to understand expectations and maintain the standard set through the relevant policy and frameworks. This should be translated effectively into policy and embedded into the procedures, practice and overall ethos of the setting. Moyles (2006) within her *Leadership Qualities Branch* suggests an effective leader or manager should be accountable through the following:

- Provide quality childcare and education services and ensure that quality assurance measures are in place (this involves having ambition, goals and strategies for continued improvement, as well as taking formal quality assurance measures).
- Understand and apply appropriate disciplinary procedures for children (this involves knowing about child psychology and the legal position of early years professionals, and having clear procedures to follow).
- Understand and apply appropriate disciplinary procedures for staff (this involves making codes of behaviour and standards for performance explicit, as well as having the necessary support programmes).
- Be able to handle complaints and other procedures that require understanding, diplomacy and tact (this involves having excellent interpersonal skills and having the ability to calm heated interaction).
- Be accountable *to* and *for* own actions and those of others (this involves being accountable *to* management committees, governing bodies, parents, etc., and accountable *for* material subjects, such as transport systems)

(Moyles 2006:38)

Activity

What do you now see as the roles and responsibilities of leaders in maintaining quality?

References

Anning, A., Cottrell, D., Frost, N., Green, J. & Robinson, M. (2006) *Developing Multiprofessional Teamwork for Integrated Children's Services*. London: Open University Press.

Aubrey, C. (2007) *Leading and Managing in the Early Years*. London: Sage.

Aubrey, C. (2011) *Leading and Managing in the Early Years* (2nd ed). London: Sage.

Belbin (2013) *Belbin Team Roles*. Available from www.belbin.com/rte.asp?id = 3.

Denscombe, M. (2007) *The Good Research Guide for Small Scale Social Research Projects* (3rd ed). Berkshire: Open University Press.

Department for Education and Skills (DfES) (2003) *Every Child Matters* (Green Paper). London: HMSO.

Department for Education and Skills (DfES) (2007) *Statutory Framework for the Early Years Foundation Stage*. Nottingham: DfES.

DfES (2007) *The Early Years Foundation Stage: Setting the Standards for Learning, Development and Care for children from birth to five*. Nottingham: DfES Publications

Families in the Foundation Years; Supporting Families in The Foundation Years (2011) Available from www.foundationyears.org.uk/2011/11/early-education-and-childcare-consultation

Miller, L., Drury, R. & Cable, C. (2012) *Extending Professional Practice in the Early Years*. London: Sage.

Moyles, J. (2006) *Effective Leadership and Management in the Early Years*. Maidenhead: Open University Press.

Mujis, D., Aubrey, C., Harris, A. & Briggs, M. (2004) How Do They Manage? A Review of the Research on Leadership in Early Childhood. *Journal of Early Childhood Research* 2(2): 157–169.

Mukherji, P. & Albon, D. (2010) *Research Methods in Early Childhood – An Introductory Guide*. London: Sage.

National College for School Leadership (NCSL) (2003) *What Leaders Read*. Available from www.inclentrust.org/uploadedbyfck/file/2%20Research%20Methodology%20(Presentations_Monographs_Guidelines)/11/effective%20leadership.pdf.

Rodd, J. (1997) Learning to be Leaders: Perceptions of Early Childhood Professionals about Leadership Roles and Responsibilities. *Early Years: An International Journal of Research and Development* 18(1): 40–44.

Rodd, J. (2004) *Leadership in Early Childhood* (2nd ed). Maidenhead: Open University Press.

Rodd, J. (2005) *Leadership: An Essential Ingredient or an Optional Extra for Quality Early Childhood Provision?* Available from www.Tactyc.Org.Uk/Pdfs/Rodd.Pdf

Rodd, J. (2006) *Leadership in Early Childhood* (3rd ed). Maidenhead: Open University Press.

Sadek, E. & Sadek, J. (2004) *Good Practice in Nursery Management* (2nd ed). Cheltenham: Nelson Thornes.

Siraj-Blatchford, I. & Manni, L. (2008) *Effective Leadership in the Early Years Sector Study*. London: Institute of Education; University of London.

Smith, A. & Langston, A. (1999) *Managing Staff in Early Years Settings*. London: Routledge.

Stacey, M. (2009) *Teamwork and Collaboration in Early Years Settings*. Exeter: Learning Matters.

Whalley, M. (2011) *Leading Practice in Early Years Settings*. London: Learning Matters.

Yates, E. & Simmons, H. (2012) *Leadership in Early Childhood: Leaders' Views on Their Role*. A Child's World: Working Together for a Better Future Conference. Aberystwyth University, Wales (June).

Index